D1553215

The Good of the Game

Recapturing Hockey's Greatness

Bruce Hood with Murray Townsend

Copyright © 1999 by Bruce Hood

All rights reserved. No part of this publication may be reproduced
or transmitted in any form or by any means, electronic or mechanical,
including photocopying, recording, or any information storage and
retrieval system, without permission in writing from the publisher.

Published in 1999 by Stoddart Publishing Co. Limited
34 Lesmill Road, Toronto, Canada M3B 2T6
180 Varick Street, 9th Floor, New York, New York 10014

Distributed in Canada by:
General Distribution Services Ltd.
325 Humber College Blvd., Toronto, Ontario M9W 7C3
Tel. (416) 213-1919   Fax (416) 213-1917
Email customer.service@ccmailgw.genpub.com

Distributed in the United States by:
General Distribution Services Inc.
85 River Rock Drive, Suite 202, Buffalo, New York 14207
Toll-free Tel. 1-800-805-1083   Toll-free Fax 1-800-481-6207
Email gdsinc@genpub.com

03   02   01   00   99   1   2   3   4   5

Canadian Cataloguing in Publication Data

Hood, Bruce
The good of the game: recapturing hockey's greatness

ISBN 0-7737-3197-0

1. Hockey. I. Townsend, Murray. II. Title.

GV847.H587 1999   796.962   C99-931451-3

Jacket design: Bill Douglas @ The Bang
Text design: Tannice Goddard

THE CANADA COUNCIL | LE CONSEIL DES ARTS
FOR THE ARTS | DU CANADA
SINCE 1957 | DEPUIS 1957

*We acknowledge for their financial support of our publishing
program the Canada Council, the Ontario Arts Council, and
the Government of Canada through the Book Publishing
Industry Development Program (BPIDP).*

Printed and bound in Canada

This book is dedicated to my mom, Hazel Hood,
who at the young age of 87 years still has
a passion for watching the games on television,
and to all of the enthusiastic hockey fans out there.

Contents

Acknowledgements   vii

Introduction: The Greatest Goal That Never
Should Have Been Scored   ix

part 1 what the kids are telling us

1 The Pure Fun of the Game   3

2 The Kids Are All Right — Then Again, Maybe
They're Not   11

3 What I Want to Be When I Grow Up   33

part 2 you wouldn't believe what I saw on the ice

4 The Goon Era   47

5 Building on the Past — The Original Six Arenas   56

6 Expansion of Consciousness   72

7 A Striped History   80

8 Official Business   92

9 Breaking Our Fighting Spirit   99

10 Rules Are Made to Be Changed   115

11 On a Breakaway — The Media, Salaries,
        Expansion, and Agents   129
12 Labour Relations — Get in the Game, Boys!   140

part 3 **in love with the game**

13 She Shoots, She Scores!   157
14 Same Game, Different Rules   165
15 The Old Skates Still Fit   175
16 Wayne Gretzky — More Than
        Just a Hockey Player   180
17 Diehards and Bandwagon Jumpers   188

part 4 **cause for hope**

18 The Top (and Bottom) 20   195
19 At the Summits and Beyond   203
20 The Game Never Stops Changing   221
21 The European Invasion   232
22 A Wake-Up Call for Hockey   249

acknowledgements

I express my thanks to the following for their encouragement and input in the writing of this book: Stoddart Publishing, for their enthusiastic support of my project, especially Angel Guerra, who masterminded it; Jim Gifford, editor and staunch hockey buff, who nursed it through its development stages; Murray Townsend, a very talented writer, who was instrumental in the success of my first book, *Calling the Shots*, and added his expertise and depth of knowledge to assist in making this one as good as it is; my wife, Daphne, who kept me at it, put up with my long hours at the computer, helped amass info, and read the copy; the staff at my travel offices for their patience and support during my absences, and for helping out with the many phone calls; and all the many folks I spoke to along the way about the book who offered me support for the concept and gave me their insights.

You have all helped make it happen, and for this I thank each of you very much.

Bruce Hood
September 1999

introduction
the greatest goal that never should have been scored

When Paul Henderson scored the most famous goal in Canadian hockey history, it might not have been such a good thing.

People look at me as if I'm crazy when I say that, but after we've talked about it a bit, I can almost see the light bulbs going on in their heads.

The Canada-Soviet series in 1972 was perhaps the biggest sporting event in Canadian history. Nothing before or since can even approach the emotion Canadians felt at the time. It was as if the Canadian players were defending everything Canada stood for. The whole country came to a standstill — televisions were brought into classrooms for games, businesses shut down, and events were cancelled if they took place during the series. Canadians who had never watched a hockey game in their lives were glued to their television sets. At my referee school in Haliburton, Ontario, we set up some old black and white televisions for the students and instructors to watch the series. Somehow, some way, everybody was watching.

Most Canadians comfortably predicted a series sweep for the Canadian team. After all, how could anybody beat us at our own game? We were the best. Always had been, always would be.

Our prediction seemed right on at first. In the opening game in Montreal on September 2, 1972, it took Canada just 30 seconds to put in the opening goal. Six minutes later, the Canadians scored another one to take a 2–0 lead. No problem.

Then we got hit with a sledgehammer. The Russians scored the next four goals and went on to a 7–3 victory.

The whole country went into a depression. How could this be? How could we have been beaten so easily at our own game? We'd find out soon enough.

The Russians showed a mastery of the fundamentals that seemed to dazzle the Canadian players, and all of us watching, as well. Their passing and skating, their play-making abilities, their dedication to teamwork — we'd never seen anyone play like they did. It was incredible.

The Canadian team redeemed itself somewhat, winning the second game, but after five games we were down three games to one (with one tie) in the best-of-eight series. The Russians needed just one more win or tie to win it all. It seemed hopeless.

What happened next became a landmark of Canadian history. We won the last three games to win the series, all in the Soviet Union, all by only one goal, all on winning goals by Paul Henderson. The last one was the most dramatic, of course. In game eight, on September 28, 1972, Henderson fired one past the outstretched glove of Vladislav Tretiak with just 34 seconds left.

To Canadians, Henderson's goal was one of those monumental occasions when you remember exactly what you were doing at the time. I watched the game with my 15-year-old son, Kevin, in the living room of our home in Milton. We danced around the room in each other's arms. We couldn't have been happier, and neither could the whole country. We were the best, and we had proven it.

But wait a second. What exactly did we prove?

When we fought back in that series, we fought against the fresh, innovative approach to hockey the Russians were showing us for the first time. We didn't win by being better hockey players. We won with heart and emotion. But we really won by intimidating the Soviets. Our players weren't as skilled as their players, and maybe not as talented, so we pushed them around, slowed them down. We found another way to win. We didn't prove our hockey supremacy in 1972. We proved that we could play rough and intimidate our opponents.

Losing the series would have given us considerable cause to examine our game more closely. Instead, we sat back after our win, content that our way of playing and training for hockey was superior, and that our boys were the best in the world. If we had lost the series, there would have been a tremendous uproar.

We would have set up government commissions to examine our approach to hockey, to find out how the better-conditioned, smoother-skating Soviets got the better of us. We would have been forced to take a close look at how we did things.

We would have discovered that we needed to emphasize skating, stickhandling, and playmaking, rather than allowing our players to simply employ the bullying tactics that have become such a predominant part of our game. Instead, the intimidation our players displayed in the Soviet series became the model for our players in the years to come, from the youngest kids just starting out to the amateur ranks, and on to the NHL. And we still think that way. If you don't believe me, look at the list of top players in the NHL. Jaromir Jagr, Peter Forsberg, Alexei Yashin, Dominik Hasek, Nicklas Lidstrom — all Europeans, all highly skilled, hard-working players. Other than a few notable exceptions (Eric Lindros and Paul Kariya come to mind) our boys simply aren't on the same level.

Most are taken aback when they first hear my suggestion that Canadian hockey would have been far better off if we'd lost that series. Then they think about it a little more, and they can't help but wonder whether an embarrassment in front of the whole world might have helped us take a giant step forward. Sure, it would have been tough at first, but we would have come out so far ahead. Just maybe our game would have changed for the better. And maybe our players would be at the same skill level as the Europeans are now.

We won the battle back in 1972, but just maybe we lost the war.

I didn't realize back in 1972 that our game was in trouble. I was too busy celebrating with the rest of the country.

In February 1998, when both Canada and the United States finished out of the medals at Nagano, I finally woke up. I realized that something is indeed wrong with the way North Americans play the game. I thought it was about time somebody took a serious look at our game to determine what's gone wrong. I wanted to tell people just how great the game of hockey used to be, and also tell them there's some good in the game today. I also wanted to let people know where our game is going on its present course, unless we take action now. That's why I wrote this book.

I have always loved hockey. As a kid, I used my older brother's skates and sticks and played on the local pond. I played on an indoor rink on natural ice. One day, I figured out what I wanted to be — a professional referee. For over 20 years, I was fortunate to be on the ice with some of the all-time greats — Howe, Hull, Beliveau, Mahovlich. During the Original Six era into the 1980s, I saw firsthand what the game was all about.

In 1988, I wrote about my career as a referee in *Calling the Shots*, which became an immediate bestseller, one of the top-selling sports books of that era. My forthright comments about the game upset a lot of people. That book was my view of the game from the ice. In this book, I look at the game not just as a former referee, but also as a fan, as someone who has been involved in the game for almost 60 years. I take a hard, honest look at what's wrong with hockey. But I also discuss what's good about the game. I reminisce about the fabulous hockey played in the Original Six era. I walk you through the early expansion years in the NHL, or the Dark Era of Hockey as I call it. I look at how the rules of the game developed, and how this affects play in today's NHL. I share some anecdotes about my time as a referee that illustrate the passion players such as Maurice Richard had for the game, and how the advent of the goon has nearly eliminated that passion. I look at what's wrong with minor hockey, and what we can do to fix it. I discuss our attitude about the game, the European influence, fighting, the greats and the not-so-greats. I talk about the people who still have a passion for the game, who play hockey just for the fun of it, and what we can learn from them. I give you the inside story on the hockey summit I attended, and how the NHL ignored our insightful suggestions.

We need to look at our game, but more importantly, we need to do something about it, now. It's imperative that we teach the young people playing the game today the skills they will need to perform at an elite level, and we need to let them have fun. Unfortunately, hockey has become a big business at the expense of the quality of play and fan interest.

I hope you enjoy my look at the past, present, and future of the greatest sport of them all. And I hope the powers that be take my suggestions seriously and put the heart back into hockey — for the good of the game.

part 1

what the kids are telling us

the pure fun of the game

1

Hockey has always been a part of my life, practically from the day I first started to walk, just as it has been for so many other young Canadian children, and in recent years, boys and girls in many other countries.

I was born in Flamborough County and grew up in the Village of Campbellville in central Ontario, located on the main line of the Canadian Pacific Railway, west of Toronto. The small burg sat where two roads crossed. There were two grocery stores, two blacksmith shops, a barbershop, a service station, a post office, a bank (part-time), one school, and some houses that led off into the surrounding farmland.

My father operated a farm on the Wheelihan property only a block from the main intersection of Campbellville. (Today, the serene countryside of those earlier farming days has been replaced by residential sprawl around this quaint village now frequented by tourists.) After a few years, my dad went to work at the local sawmill, so we moved from the farm to the house closest to the corner. From our kitchen window I could see if any of my friends were at the corner; I could speed out the back door with some kind of hockey stick in hand hoping to get into a game of hockey on the road at the corner, in summer or winter.

Sometimes we played under one of the few streetlights in the village, if the early winter darkness had set in. But most often, we had our ponds, our home away from home in both summer and winter for all the kids from the area. In the summer, we swam in the pond and built rafts. But in the winter, the pond became action central for all us would-be NHLers.

The sawmill needed a lot of water to operate, so there were three ponds. Only the main pond froze over well enough to play hockey on, and even then the water still ran where it entered and left the pond, so we had to be careful.

Once the pond started to freeze, we'd check it constantly until the day finally came when we could skate on it. We couldn't get home from school fast enough to get our skates and hockey sticks. We didn't have shin pads or hockey gloves. Usually we just wore overalls and winter jackets and mitts. The odd kid might have a Toronto Maple Leafs or Montreal Canadiens sweater, but those were rare. Anything would do for a puck, and I do mean anything. Some people called horse droppings "road apples," but we called them pucks, if we gave them a day or two to freeze. To us, the NHL was about as far away as Mars.

We played hockey from after school until suppertime, even though it had long since become dark. The only light came from the few street lamps a couple of hundred feet away up an embankment, unless there was a full moon.

We played hockey throughout the weekends, morning till night. The weather would have to be extremely bad for us to stop playing (we'd pretty much have to lose feeling in our fingers and toes). Snow could be a problem, too, but only a temporary one. We often spent our lunch hours on school days clearing the pond of snow and would sometimes be late getting back to class for the afternoon. Even worse, after school more often than not our older brothers would take over the pond we had just cleared off. (Things probably haven't changed much in that respect.) Most of the time, though, everybody could play, even our sisters, if we could convince them that standing between two large chunks of ice and having pucks shot at them was an important job.

We would scrape the snow back with shovels or whatever else we could find and pile it in banks high along the sides to make a rink in the middle of the frozen pond. The puck rarely strayed beyond the piles of snow. Nobody had ever heard of slapshots or curved sticks in those days. The object of the game was to stickhandle up the ice and pass the puck only when there were too many opponents trying to take it from you. It was a simple way to play.

Somewhere along the way we began to wear different types of padding. We'd strap old catalogues to our knees with pieces of leather from horse harnesses. Anybody who managed to get a pair of hand-me-down hockey gloves was looked on with envy.

Hockey didn't stop if the pond wasn't ready. The road in the centre of the village did just as well. There weren't many cars anyway, in those days, but there were plenty of horses.

When I was 11, my family moved from Campbellville to nearby Milton. They had a pond there, too, but even better, they had an indoor arena. What a thrill the arena was for me, with its proper boards, player boxes, and everything, just like in the NHL. The arena had natural ice because few small towns had ice-making refrigeration devices in their arenas in those days.

I was still in a small town, but to me, I was already in the big leagues. I got to play on an actual team and discovered for the first time how many kids were actually supposed to be on the ice at one time, among other rules. If it warmed up outside, the ice at the arena became too soft, and we couldn't play our league games. All week, I'd look forward to those games, and if we couldn't play, I'd be devastated.

In Milton and nearby Acton, Georgetown, and Oakville, I moved up through various levels of hockey: midget, junior, and intermediate. I played defence, with my size my biggest asset. I wasn't a very good stickhandler. Come to think of it, I wasn't a very good playmaker either. Usually I just banged the puck up the boards when I got it. (I play old-timer hockey now, and while I'm no better now than I was then, at least I can make the odd good play.)

I was a rough-and-tumble type of player, maybe even a little dirty. I didn't mind using my elbows and the referees didn't mind giving me a lot of penalties. I think the rough way I played as a kid helped me out during my refereeing career later on — I knew all the dirty tricks to look out for.

Hockey in those days was so different than it is now. We stickhandled. We passed the puck around and made solid body checks. The puck mostly stayed on the ice, unless someone hoisted it to get it out of our end. There were no slapshots, so the goalies didn't need face masks. We checked in the lower body area, and there were no helmets. I'm sure a helmet would have been a good idea for the odd time we fell and hit our heads on the ice (which I did the odd time), but generally, no protection was needed for the way the game was played. We always played for the puck and made contact only when trying to regain possession. High sticking or elbowing to the upper body and head area was not as common as it is today. Rarely did anyone get their stick up around other players' heads. We focused on the game itself, on having fun.

When I think about how we played hockey when I was a boy, I relive the pure and simple pleasure of that time. My friends and I all had dreams, of course, of one day playing in the NHL, but that's not why we laced up our skates by the frozen pond or played on the road at the centre of town. We just loved playing hockey. We fell in love with the game when we were young, and it became a part of us.

It's different for the young kids of today. They have so many kinds of entertainment to choose from, so many distractions. If it's a little chilly outside, they can stay indoors and play video games, or rent a movie, or flip through the dozens of channels on their TVs. Or they can play games on their computers, or surf the Internet. We had far fewer options when I was a boy, which is why hockey became such a big part of my life. The kids today are missing out on the simple pleasure we found in hockey.

You can still drive around any Canadian town and see a road hockey game in action, but even that's changed. Oh sure, there is probably still the odd rickety old goalie net covered with tattered webbing that's dragged out onto the street by kids who have worn-out sticks and running shoes, makeshift goalie pads that have seen better days, and beat-up tennis balls. But more often nowadays the net is top quality, with fine mesh. The players have good quality sticks, which are made of wood or aluminum. They're wearing the latest in in-line skates, and they use only official road hockey balls.

The ponds and rivers don't seem to freeze over as they once did. (We could probably blame global warming and pollution for that.) Where I live, people don't make backyard rinks as much as they used to, either. They aren't up for putting in a lot of work only to have it disappear during a warm day. We've lost some of the sense of community we had when we put a lot of effort into getting ready to play hockey, even if the fun lasted only a short time.

Today, kids play hockey year-round, in arena complexes that

have as many as eight ice pads. The hockey is extremely structured, and the schedules can be gruelling. During the winter,
some rep teams play two or three games and practise a few
times a week, and then journey to tournaments on the weekends. When they get home, the kids don't pick up their sticks
and head for a pond. They do anything else but play hockey.

The travel, the coaching, the money spent on their equipment
and ice time all place tremendous pressure on our kids to be
good at the game. They have to work hard to improve to keep
up with the other kids. They likely want to be promoted to a
higher level of hockey (or at least that's what their parents
would have them think).

I wonder if the true spirit of the game exists for youngsters
in this environment. They should be able to get out on that
ice and just have fun chasing down a loose puck, like the
pros do when they come out to do their warm-up before their
games, before they begin their drills. Handling the puck, dipsy-
doodling with the puck, and trying new things may not come
naturally to them at first. But these tactics help develop talent,
which doesn't show through in today's structured defensive
game. The parents pay a lot for their kids to play hockey, and
they want results. Often, the parents play hockey vicariously
through their kids. Is there additional incentive for kids to play
like the pros do when they read about the unbelievable salaries
the players receive?

I'm not trying to say that kids no longer love to play hockey

— of course many do. But they're missing out on what makes hockey so great: the pure fun of the game. Hockey is so structured now that the fun seems to have been lost along the way. A bunch of kids choosing sides, dropping a puck, and just going at it, all for the love of the game. What could be better than that?

the kids are all right — then again, maybe they're not

2

I t used to be very simple. Saturday mornings, fathers would drop off their sons at the arena for their once-a-week game. Maybe the dads would watch from the stands with a hot cup of coffee in their hands, or maybe they'd go home and come back later to pick up their kids. It was a father-son ritual. Mothers didn't go to the games that often.

The parents didn't scream at the coaches or players. They'd just cheer and offer advice to their kids. Of course, they still yelled at the referees — that's been a tradition since the start of hockey.

If a boy played on a rep team it meant he played a second

game per week and had an additional practice. It meant some added dedication to the game for the child, but the key was that kids were playing against other players at their own talent level rather than kids who were more skilled than they were, which was best for the kid and the parents.

In Canada, there weren't nearly as many arenas or ice pads as there are now. Kids spent their free time playing road and pond hockey. They couldn't get enough hockey, and they wanted more. When the last game of the season was over, the skates, sticks, and equipment were put away until the following fall. The kids would turn to other interests during that time and mostly forget about hockey.

The good old days of hockey are over, unfortunately. Hockey is a very different game today. There have been advancements in pads and skates; there are more arenas and more leagues. But the game isn't necessarily better because of these changes.

Nowadays, a child playing for a rep team commits to his team for a calendar year, especially if he plays AAA. (AAA is the highest talent classification of minor hockey in Canada, followed by AA, A, B, and so on.) These kids not only play hockey during the fall and winter, they attend hockey camps, skating drill schools, and other organized events during the summer — anything to help them learn. They practically live the sport year-round.

There are those for whom a hockey camp is just a vacation, something to do until school starts again. These players go every year and experience no real increase in the quality of their play. If they are content to attend the camp simply for the fun of it, fine, as long as it doesn't decrease their interest in playing the sport during the winter.

I'm a big believer in kids taking part in other activities after the hockey season is over, the way kids used to. They should be playing lacrosse, baseball, tennis, roller hockey, and soccer. It allows them a break, and playing the other sports can actually make them better hockey players in the fall. Even the players at the top professional level don't play hockey all year long. They need a break, a cooling off period, away from the sport. They expend a lot of energy, intensity, and emotion to be at the top of their game all the time. Few can maintain that pace for an extended period. The kids need to remember that they play hockey for the fun of it. At their age, hockey shouldn't be a job. If it is, they'll miss out on the kinds of things kids do, and their social lives can suffer. Kids in their teens need to experience a healthy cross-section of activities — hobbies, summer camp, part-time jobs — if they wish to fully develop their lives as a whole, and to be better at everything they do.

Wayne Gretzky agrees with me on this one. He played baseball during the summers. Most of today's veteran NHL players played other sports and took part in other activities in the off-season. Detroit Red Wing Brendan Shanahan and Joe Nieuwendyk of the Dallas Stars played competitive lacrosse, and they often say how much that experience has helped them in their hockey careers. In fact, they're still involved in lacrosse and donate their time to help promote the sport and help out young kids.

I've witnessed first-hand how great lacrosse is for kids. I have enjoyed being a guest referee at an annual celebrity fund-raising lacrosse game that is played in a different community in Ontario each year. They get an excellent turnout of professional hockey players for those games, and those players are all excellent lacrosse players as well. It's a real treat to watch these guys play lacrosse when I'm used to seeing them skating up and down the ice with a hockey stick. This fine group of athletes appreciates where they came from and want to give back to the community.

Instead of taking a break from hockey and trying out new things, our hockey system forces kids today to stay on top of their game year-round. If they want to stay competitive, they have to do what the other kids are doing or risk falling behind. If one team works out all summer, the other teams have to follow suit. If a kid knows that his friends are improving their skills at summer hockey camp, his parents have no choice but to send him there, too, if they want him to stay at the same level or eventually move up.

Hockey is no longer just a winter sport. In Ontario, teams hold their tryouts in the spring, right after the end of the season. That way, they can spend the summer improving as a team. Almost all rep teams in Ontario have some kind of summer program where they participate as a team. And if a child is on an AAA team in particular, he has little time to do anything else over the summer.

Of course, there's nothing wrong with kids improving their hockey skills during the summer. They have more time than they do during the winter, when they're playing in tournaments and attending school. The referee school I held in the summers was the only opportunity budding young referees had to improve their skills outside of a game situation. But now there are hockey schools for goalies, defencemen, and forwards, and for improving skating, shooting, conditioning, body-checking, and just about any aspect of the game you can think of. We've gone overboard. The kids' skills will improve, but their mind, body, and soul may suffer.

Running a rep minor hockey team is like running a business — it costs a lot of money. You wouldn't believe how much it actually costs for a group of kids to play organized hockey.

The following is a budget for an AAA peewee team (peewee players turn 12 during the year they play to qualify).

Sales and Marketing Revenue Forecast

Item	Costs	Item	Revenue
a) Summer Costs		League assmnt. @ $765	$13,000
M/J x 14 practices *	$1,739	Summer assmnt @ $370	$6,290
14 instructor *	$1,400	Apparel @ $260	$4,420
Jul/Aug. prac. x 19 *	$1,925	Tournaments @ $250	$4,250
4 instructor *	$400	Referees @ $150	$2,550
Sept. practices x 6 *	$745	**Sub Total Player Assmnt.**	$30,510
b) Winter Costs		Bags donated	$1,500
League ice/fees *	$13,000	(Total cost per player $1,785)	
Tournaments *	$4,250		
Apparel *	$4,296	**Fund-raising target**	$15,821
Bags *	$1,500		
Team exp./admin. ++	$4,000	**Potential fund-raising ++**	

Sales and Marketing Revenue Forecast (cont'd)

Item	Costs	Item	Revenue
Referee x 25 *	$2,500	Golf tournament	$8,000
Additional ice 25 wks x 2 ++	$8,026	Program	$6,000
Winter instructor ++	$2,000	Gate admission & event	$1,000
Goalie instructor ++	$1,200	Hockey pool	$3,500
Team party/rsrve. ++	$850	Player sponsorship x $150	$2,500
Total Costs	**$47,831**	Team sponsorship	$2,500
* Incl. in Player Assessment		Tournament	$4,000
++ To Be Funded		Pet food, bottle drive Etc.	$3,000

Detailed Budget Costs

1. Summer Ice

a) May – Thurs. and Sun. 6 hours x $124.15/hr. = $745
b) June – Thurs. and Sun. 8 hours x $124.15/hr. = $994
c) July – Thurs. and Sun. 7 hours shared at 50% or $62.07/hr = $435
d) August – 12 hours total at $124.15/hr = $1,490
e) May – Instructor 6 hours x $100 = $600
f) June – Instructor 8 hours x $100 = $800
g) August – Instructor 4 hours x $100/hr. = $400
h) September – Ice 6 hours x $124.15/hr. = $745

2. League Winter Ice

Includes one home game (Tues.) and one practice per week (Thurs.)
September 20th – March 20th = $13,000

3. Additional Winter Ice

25 Saturdays October 2 – March 25 (includes break for Christmas) at
 four rinks at $160.50 per hour = $4,013
25 Weeknights October 2 – March 25 at $160.50 per hour (TBA) = $4,013

4. Winter Instructors

20 sessions at $100 per session = $2,000
Goalie sessions 6 per goalie (12 x $100) = $1,200

Detailed Budget Costs (continued)

---

5. Tournaments
8 tournaments at $500 per tournament = $4,250

6. Referees and Time Keepers
Based on 16 league games and 9 playoff games at $100 per game = $2,500

7. Team Administrative Expenses = $4,000
Coach's allowance $2,500
Bus $750
Phone costs $500
Photocopies $250

6. Referees and Time Keepers = $4,296
Jackets – $172.50
Practice jerseys at $28.75
Coach's warm-up suits $185.00

6. Team Party and Reserve = $850

Kind of blows your mind, doesn't it? Almost $50,000 to run a hockey team of seventeen 12-year-olds! This is just an average, too. Other teams incur even higher expenses. And believe it or not, some teams even pay their coaches. Many teams raise money to pay for a season of hockey through fund-raising, but usually the parents still shell out a lot of money for their kids. What the parents pay varies because fund-raising never covers the full cost. A season of minor hockey can cost thousands of dollars in fees, as well as extra costs for hotel stays during tournaments, equipment, gate fees, travel expenses — you name it. It can cost these parents a small fortune.

The cost of minor hockey could very well be where all the trouble with parents began. If they're laying out that kind of dough, they sure as heck want to get their money's worth. They're not likely going to sit back and just accept whatever goes on. They want to know exactly what they're paying for, and if they have any kind of problem you can be sure everyone will hear about it. Parents spend a lot of time talking to each other. They're often at the rink almost an hour before the game starts and a half hour after it finishes. At practices, they have close to two hours to kill while waiting. There's little else for them to do but talk to each other, so the costs of kids' hockey and the value they are getting (or not getting) is often the topic. Parents especially like to discuss costs if their child is not doing as well as hoped.

Of course, it's good that parents take an interest in what their kids are doing. But in the case of minor hockey, it goes too far. Many of us have seen some of the crazy things that go on at minor hockey games: parents fighting with each other and the coaches, police getting involved, parents yelling at kids on both teams, and, of course, parents yelling at referees.

That last point has always been a sore spot with me. If a kid sees that his parents don't respect the people in charge of the game, then he's not going to either. Most of the time the parents are wrong, anyway. They show no respect for the referee. But when the players get out of hand on the ice, the referee is the first to get blamed. *He didn't have control of the game,* they say. Remember, these kids will eventually become parents, too, and the cycle of abuse of referees and coaches will continue. A friend of mine helps out in the penalty box at minor league games. He says that players as young as 10 years old routinely swear at the referee so loudly that the referee is bound to hear it.

As I said, because the game has become so expensive, parents have become more involved because they want to see where their money goes. And it isn't just hockey. Parents are much more involved overall in their kids' lives now. (And that's a good thing.) But for some reason parents feel that it's their responsibility to stick up for their kids, even when they don't need any help. If they see their kid facing any kind of injustice, they're in there fighting for them, rather than letting the kids handle it themselves. They're trying to help out, but really they're interfering, and not letting the experts do their job or the kids find their own way. Of course, the more parents *think* they know about something, the more likely they are to find fault with it. I believe that's what's happened with Canadians and hockey.

This interference is occurring in rep hockey and in house leagues. One Saturday morning I ventured into a local arena in Oakville, Ontario, to watch a friend's young son play. He had been telling me for quite some time how exciting it was and how much fun it was to watch the kids play. The game took place in a new complex that houses four ice rinks, so there was a lot of minor hockey being played that morning. All the rinks featured little guys giving it their best. I wandered around until I found where my friend's child was playing. I stood and watched from a distance for a while as the kids made their way up and down the ice, and then off on the three-minute buzzer.

Thank goodness for that automatic buzzer. It sounds a stop in play, and it's compulsory for the coaches to change the lines so that every player on the team gets a chance to play. Otherwise I'm sure a high percentage of coaches would sit some of the less-talented players and go for it, using their biggest and best players all the time, just for that almighty win. It's human nature, this push to win no matter what the emotional cost to the other players on the team, and it can cost them dearly.

I enjoyed watching these eight- and nine-year-olds race around the ice and chase the puck. I also observed the parents. I was amazed at their poses, their shouting, and their antics. It was really quite interesting. When my boys were kids, I hardly ever got to see them play minor hockey because I was on the road refereeing during most winters and I often wonder how I would have acted had I been able to attend their games. Would I be like some of those I have seen who lose it at the ice rink? Or would I have been the level-headed type I was as a referee? I like to think I would have been on my best behaviour. During one winter later in my career, a friend of mine and I coached a house-league minor hockey team. The team played Monday nights (I was usually home on those nights because in those days there were few Monday night games in the NHL). This past summer a coach of one of the other teams in the league at the time came up to me and told me an interesting story of when his team played mine. The team he was coaching was down 5–1 to mine when he decided to move his best player from defence to forward. The move worked, and his team went on to win the game. This coach reminded me that after our team lost, I went out of my way to come over and shake his hand for a coaching job well done. Maybe I would have acted the same way as a father watching my kids play.

When watching my friend's child play, I found it startling that few of the parents seemed happy with how their kids were playing the game. Sometimes they'd holler, "Check him! Check him! Skate! Skate! Shoot! Shoot!" Or they'd shout, "Oh, you missed him!" or "Come on, ref, get in the game!" or "Get up! Get up!" and so on. Sometimes the fathers, and sometimes the mothers, would climb up onto the boards so they could shout their "instructions" over the high glass.

One father kept running along the open walkway behind the glass. He'd follow the play as it moved up the ice, almost as if he were in the play too. As he ran he'd shout, "Skate! Check! Shoot!"

I was surprised to hear few positive comments from the parents. I expected them to support their kids, to shout "Good skating! Good shooting!" or "Way to go, Bobby! Good play!" Nobody really seemed to be enjoying themselves at the game, except for a few mothers who sat up at the back and chatted away with each other, casting the odd glance toward the ice, and offering a quick clap or an occasional enthusiastic shout. They were so busy socializing, they weren't aware of what their kids (or their husbands) were doing.

I was even more astounded when I watched the parents and kids leave the arena as the games would finish. I found it hard to tell in many instances which team had won the game, as the parents all seemed to be saying things such as "You missed that shot," or "Boy, they were all over you guys," and so forth. Most of their comments were negative. I didn't see much of parents putting their arms around the kids' shoulders, smiling, saying, "Way to go," so that everybody, not just the kids, could leave the rink with a good feeling about themselves and life in general. It was such a lost opportunity for the parents to positively participate in a fun sport with their children. It made me wonder what this game of hockey is all about.

●

For all that needs to be changed about minor hockey, much needs to remain the same. I think there's a lot of good about kids' hockey, and that good needs to be recognized and celebrated.

At any minor hockey game you'll hear the parents yelling at their kids instead of shouting support, but that's not entirely what minor hockey is all about — it just seems that way. Parents, coaches, players, and referees seem to just accept this kind of behaviour and think that it's all part of the process. It's the people who don't have kids or haven't had kids in minor hockey that seem the most outraged by this nonsense. They just see the bad, not the good.

This statement appeared on the budget I showed you earlier:

Coach's Philosophy
First and foremost I want the players to develop better skills. Not only hockey skills, but life skills. I feel many of the mental skills you need to be successful in sports also apply to everyday life — discipline, motivation and focus.

People don't know about this kind of positive approach when they criticize minor hockey, about all the good that hockey can do for a child as a person. If you know any kids who are heavily involved in hockey, I'm sure you're delighted about the kind of people they are. They show respect for their elders. They've learned invaluable social skills and have developed strong self-esteem. They've learned responsibility and discipline, motivation and focus. They've become the people described in this coach's philosophy.

Sportswriters are always saying that hockey players are the most cooperative of all the professional athletes, that they're some of the friendliest people they've met. Hockey players learn how to be that way in large part from playing hockey as kids. The camaraderie of the dressing room and of backing up their teammates and taking pride in their abilities is irreplaceable. The discipline they learn helps them beyond the arenas, in school, in their jobs, and in their personal lives.

Minor hockey coaches have a great deal to do with how these children become such respected adults. But all people hear about are the bad people in the game such as Graham James, who was convicted of sexual abuse of junior hockey players. Or they hear about the verbally abusive coaches who make the news for their antics.

People don't realize that the vast majority of coaches are good people who have only the kids' best interests at heart. And why wouldn't they? They're volunteers, remember, and they contribute a lot of their free time, which means they also spend a considerable amount of time away from their families. They coach because they think they can do a good job and can help the kids. It's the same with any sport. But they're human, and they make mistakes, like anyone else. Many, many mistakes.

Part of the process to correct that is a coach's certification program, which is a requirement for Ontario rep teams. There are different levels of certification, similar to referees, who must also work their way up to the level of the games they officiate. The excellent coaching program has really developed over many years. But if these coaches are being trained to teach young players only defensive hockey, how can the kids' skills be improved? We need to change the way the coaches think, the way they teach. They need to teach our kids how to play the puck rather than to stop opposing players from playing it. The governing coaching bodies should legislate proper coaching systems, including how to play offence. Those coaches who adopt sneaky tricks to take advantage of the rules should be banned from the game.

All coaches have their good points and their bad points. It's the same for any person walking down the street. But because of the pressure on coaches from the parents, the coaches are expected to be perfect. That's impossible. (Referees are expected to be perfect, too, which is much closer to reality — if you ask a referee.)

Coaches shoulder a lot of responsibility. They're expected to make the kids better hockey players, and if they don't, the parents become angry. The coaches are expected to treat the kids properly, be good role models, and on top of everything else,

they're expected to *win*. And if they don't win, or if the kids
misbehave, the coaches take much of the blame. It's not un-
common for parents to mutiny against the coach, and go to
the team's association to try to have that coach ousted. Often, the
coach resigns out of frustration, or is replaced if the parents have
convinced the association that the team needs a new coach.

Most parents do not blame themselves for their kids' lack of
discipline in hockey. To them, it's always the coach's fault. If
they can't control the players they shouldn't be coaching. These
parents should take a hard look at themselves before they start
blaming the coach. If they look around the stands at the other
parents showing lack of control, what do they expect their kids
to do on the ice?

●

Everybody wants to win. In fact, they want to win so much
they can sometimes forget that hockey is supposed to be fun.
The burden of responsibility is too much, even for the coach.
They're forced to stringently structure their training program,
or the parents believe they're not doing their job. Some coaches
are even ridiculed if they try to make practice fun. Parents often
don't see that if their kids are having a good time, they become
more inspired to succeed, and that they need a break from the
rigours of skating and passing and shooting. All the parents
want to see is results.

As I've said before, many people forget or don't seem to
realize that playing hockey is supposed to be fun. I think of the

days I spent just playing hockey all day long on the pond in Campbellville as fun. Those are some of my fondest memories, and I know that that experience had a lot to do with me becoming the person I am today. We need to get the fun back in the game.

I'll admit that it's difficult to get the perfect balance between fun and learning the skills necessary to excel at the game of hockey. But the best coaches can incorporate fun into their programs and still teach the kids what they need to know. Some coaches think that the fun of hockey isn't the experience, but in winning alone. I even heard one coach tell his players recently that hockey is not supposed to be fun.

You will very rarely see a team have a scrimmage in practice any more. Scrimmages are now considered a waste of time. The kids spend most of their time practising drills aimed at improving their skills. The games are for improving game skills. Of course, drills are important, and in recent years their value has increased because there is less wasted time at practices, but I really think there's too much of an emphasis on drills and not enough time on just having fun. The players accept that they're going to work hard at practices. They know that it's a part of the process.

It used to be that one coach would come out onto the ice with a pail full of pucks and dump them out. All of the kids spent lots of time stickhandling and manoeuvring about, shooting on the net and generally having fun, while at the same time getting a good feel for the puck. The kids would take part in three-on-two drills, and would line up to take shots on the goalie. At the end of practice, the kids would be rewarded by a scrimmage — a fun game after the hard work they put in practising. If coaches reserved part of the practice time to let the kids enjoy a fun exercise, I think that they would even enjoy some of the more mundane drills. Kids love competing against each other. If a coach is smart, he can merge fun and working hard so they can learn skills as they enjoy themselves. Sometimes it's best not to worry if the kids are learning, but be satisfied that they're having fun.

Now at practices the kids work on so many plays — breakout plays, positioning to shut down breakouts, cross-ice passes from one zone to the other to open up the ice, and, conversely, all the necessary moves to defend against wide-open play. They learn how to take a guy out in front of the net (always verging on breaking the rules), how to check in the corners. It's a different world now, and the kids simply aren't getting out of hockey what they used to.

It's not unusual for a coach to threaten to "skate" his team in practice after his team has put in a poor game performance. Generally, a coach makes his team endure one straight hour of skating, nonstop. That kind of punishment for poor play is too much for young players. I know of at least one team that did that until the players were throwing up in the benches.

Coaches all have different philosophies, of course. Some

think that pushing the players will ensure that they give the most they've got, and that the experience will be good for them in the long run. They're the types who believe that hockey is not fun. Those kinds of coaches scare me. At the same time, if the coach doesn't push the kids and they don't win, the coach is blamed for not bearing down on them. Parents are fickle. If the coach pushes too hard, they don't like it. If the coach doesn't push hard enough, they don't like that, either. The key is to find some kind of balance.

European coaches believe that practices are much more important than the games, that the games are secondary. Their system appears to be working, so why aren't we following their model? The Europeans are better skaters and stickhandlers. Canadians and Americans are much better in high-pressure situations — they show the heart and desire necessary to win. That's what we're seeing when less skilled North American players go out and beat a more talented European team. Canadian junior teams frequently win the world championship with dedication and desire, though they're obviously overmatched in skill.

●

The minor hockey leagues and organizations are well aware of the problems that exist in kids' hockey. They generally try hard to fix them, though it's often a trial-and-error process. In recent years the Ontario Minor Hockey Association (OMHA) has had the players shake hands with the other team before the game, and to shake hands with the other team's coaches. The referees shake hands with the coaches before the game. It helps the refs to realize that they're watching over real people, and I think it makes a difference in the way they call the game.

During the 1980s, I was involved in the Fair Play in Sport Commission for Canada, established by the federal government in response to the many complaints by Canadians about the win-at-all-costs attitude Canadian athletes were demonstrating at the time. Its purpose was to encourage fair play, acknowledge it, and reward it appropriately. You might have heard Don Cherry making fun of "those Fair Play guys and their desire for cutesy play" on "Coach's Corner" on *Hockey Night in Canada*. I don't know why he mocks such an important forum on fair play. Does he not want our kids to play safely and fairly?

The Fair Play Commission instituted some good programs in the school system in an attempt to get our kids to think differently at an early age. I'm sure that our recommendations affected many children, but it's hard to know how many. The message we delivered needs to be supported and carried on by others. The commission, which still exists, deals with more than just fair play now, focusing on ethics of Canadian sports.

●

Believe it or not, there are few fights in minor hockey. The players risk getting kicked out of the game and face suspensions. The NHL could well learn from minor hockey on this one. The league claims to be serious about getting rid of fighting, but they never seem to get around to it.

But though there isn't much fighting, there is a lot of violence at the minor league level. The kids have hockey sticks in hand and know a host of dirty tricks to get back at an opponent aside from dropping the gloves. They place their sticks in just the right place on an opponent at a face-off to restrict movement, to upset that player and get him off his game mentally. They push against other players along the boards after the whistle blows for a few extra seconds, for the same reason. They grab hold of an opponent's stick or jersey just enough to restrict his movement and break his concentration, but not enough to receive a penalty. These types of actions upset other players, who in turn use their sticks and elbows to retaliate, or even throw a punch with a gloved fist.

Organizations institute rules to curb violent behaviour. Their attempts to cut back on the violence are not always successful, but I'm glad to see the organizations recognize that there is a problem. In organized hockey, the mindset is "You change first and I'll follow." So even if we start today, it will take a while to change the way we think about minor hockey, and to see the implications that those changes would have for the NHL. We need the NHL stars — the Gretzkys, the Kariyas — to speak up about the need to increase the quality of our kids' skills so that they'll be able to compete when they reach the big leagues. Kariya, for one, leads by example. He skates and shoots on a level with the elite Europeans, and his conditioning is impressive. But he and others need to tell those who play, coach, and manage the game in this country that improving our kids' skills is paramount, and that we risk being knocked even farther down the world rankings in hockey if we don't begin to fix what's wrong now.

In house-league hockey, a team will play a 16-game schedule with 14 players on a team. Each kid gets about seven two-minute shifts in a game, with a practice every three or four weeks, usually at six in the morning. This is not much of an opportunity for these kids to learn a whole lot. Without the casual play on a local pond or outdoor rink, where they can go out and just play hockey and hone their skills, there's not much chance for the average player to develop. I think that because the kids don't get much time on the ice in organized play, it's easier for coaches to teach simpler systems — the neutral zone trap, the left-side lock, or whatever you want to call it. They learn little to do with puck handling, but instead use their bodies and sticks to shut down the other players.

Professional hockey is not much better at giving ample time to learn the skills, either. The top player on the ice for a team in professional hockey — usually the number one centre — may handle the puck for less than a minute over an entire game. The less talented players on the ice, such as those on the third or fourth line, will get even less ice time. The defencemen, who are intent on just dumping the puck out of their zone or into their opponents', do not handle the puck much, and their offensive skills suffer.

As in minor hockey, if a team plays a lot of games but has few practices, they will not develop into better players. Instead, they'll continue to play the physical, intimidating, chippy style we have come to accept in our game, for which Canadians are best known.

Maybe it's time that the coaches in minor hockey put away their win-at-all-costs attitude and let the kids have fun in playing the game. We need to allow them to make mistakes, to be creative with the puck, and play scrimmages. If the kids play to 9–7 finals, what's the harm?

what I want to be
when I grow up

3

During the 1997–98 hockey season, I watched a play-off game between two pretty good rival Tier II junior teams in Ontario, the Oakville Blades and the Milton Merchants. I had mixed emotions in going to the game. I live in Oakville, but I was also formerly a long-time resident of Milton. I had grown up playing hockey in Milton, from minor up to senior (where we played against Oakville). I also started my officiating career in Milton, and went to the NHL from there. And Milton is still the location of the main office of my travel agency network. But for the past 10 years I have lived on Lake Ontario in the Village of Bronte, a suburb of

Oakville, where I have another two travel office locations. So I didn't go to the game to cheer for one side or the other. And I wasn't there as a retired NHL referee. I just wanted to enjoy watching some kids play hockey.

Fat chance of that. From the very beginning of the game, I couldn't believe what I was seeing — high sticking, spearing, head hunting in the corners, and punching in the face while play was going on, in full view of the fans and the referee.

Every time a player headed toward the net, he and the defending player would bring up their sticks, and they'd nearly cross-check each other in the face. I saw the same kind of rough play in the corner, at the blueline, and at centre ice. The kids played this hard, intimidating style as if they'd always played hockey that way, as if it was the accepted way to play the game. Their goal was to stymie smooth play by using their sticks, arms, hands, or whatever they could to stop the other players from getting loose and skating with the puck. They spent about 10 percent of their playing time worrying about what to do with the puck, or getting into position to take a pass or make a play, or being creative with the puck. They spent the rest of their time slowing down, hacking, and intimidating opposing players. I even saw a Milton player charge an Oakville player into the boards from behind, and while that player was down, he cross-checked him across the back of the neck and gave him a couple of punches for good measure — atrocious behaviour, on the ice or anywhere else.

Just before the period ended, two players stood within two feet of the referee, their sticks in each other's faces making contact, almost as if duelling. They high sticked each other while play continued and moved up the ice away from the area of combat. Their antics continued for several seconds. They took a couple of final chops at each other and decided to get back into the play. This type of behaviour went on throughout the game and was obviously an accepted part of the game, judging by the way the ref handled it. He observed the players doing this, yelled at them, and let three of four fouls occur on the play. I hadn't seen a junior game for about a year, and I had hoped the games had been cleaned up from the last time I had been to one. But in fact the amount of rough play was worse.

I looked around at other people watching the game. No fans or parents seemed to be fazed by any of the rough play in the least. Apparently what they were seeing was normal conduct for a junior hockey game. I was surprised at these people for not being outraged by the somewhat brutal play. For the kids, it was just the accepted way to play. What a shame.

The interesting part about the game was that when all this garbage wasn't taking place, it was an entertaining game to watch. These youngsters could fly on their skates, showed some impressive playmaking skills, and had dynamite shots. It's too bad they didn't have the chance to show their stuff that often.

I went down to the referee's dressing room between periods to say hello to the referee, a chap who lived in a city not too far away and whom I had met in my involvement in hockey. We chatted for a while and talked about the game. Then he said, "Can you believe what those kids are doing to each other out there?" I was astonished as much by his question as I was by what I saw on the ice. I was at least satisfied that he, too, didn't seem to agree with what was taking place in the game. He was just going with the flow. I didn't know if he wanted to change the style of the game by calling penalties and setting a different standard. I was reminded of when I'd referee Philadelphia Flyer games. The players operated on the edge all the time, continually testing the referee while intimidating their opponents. It sure wasn't up to one person in a striped jersey to try to change the game in that era, and apparently it wasn't that way at this junior game as well.

There was also a supervisor of officials in the room. He had a pad with notes written all over it — it's his job to note the work of the referee and linesmen and report back to the league office. I would love to have seen his notes. I'm sure he hadn't written a thing about what I saw as very serious offences on the ice. Why not? Well, as my referee friend had said, it was just the way the game is played today.

I find it hard to believe what is accepted now as hockey at that level. And I'm glad I don't get to too many junior games any more.

●

I remember a father telling me about the time he dropped his boys off at the local arena on a Friday night to watch a junior game. It was family night, so all the kids in town were invited to attend the game for a minimal charge. The father went off to attend another function.

When he returned to pick up the boys later, police cars, with lights flashing, were parked at the doors of the arena. There had been a first-class brawl on the ice that had boiled over into the stands. This father decided then and there that neither he nor his boys would be back. His two sons played minor hockey and enjoyed being involved, and their pop sure didn't want to have them think that the way the juniors played was the right way. He didn't want to discourage them so early in their careers.

I wonder how many good young players with a lot of potential never play at a level beyond kids' hockey because of what they see at the next level up, and at what they see taking place in the NHL. Surveys show that as many as 40 percent of kids choose not to move up in organized hockey because of the abuse they face and the risk of potential injury. And nothing is going to change about the way we plan and think about the game unless we speak up.

The big problem with junior hockey, why there is little effort to develop skills and sportsmanship, is that the NHL provides a poor model for our youth. Why would our kids play any differently when they see how the NHL game is played? They watch players in the NHL fight and illegally use their sticks, and they don't see an emphasis on skills and speed (at least from the Canadian players).

Jeff Kugel, a 6'7" 260-pound player for the Windsor Spitfires of the Ontario Hockey League (OHL), obviously used the NHL style as a model for his play. The Michigan native watched NHL players batter and high stick each other — what he believed he had to do to get noticed and make it to the NHL. He went on a rampage during a game in the fall of 1998, creating a nightmare for himself, for the league, and for hockey in general.

Kugel left the bench during the game, and while there was a stoppage in play with some activity already taking place on the ice, he headed for opposing players and went nuts. He made a complete fool of himself, skating around and throwing punches at every opponent he thought he could catch, challenging the visiting team's bench, and creating mayhem. His antics received television coverage around the globe, attention that neither the league nor the game wanted or needed.

The OHL, the top level of junior hockey and the most common stepping stone to the NHL, took a dim view of Kugel's rampage. They gave him a lifetime suspension from the league and asked all other junior leagues to honour it.

Kugel was asked to pay the price for his actions, but really, the incident wasn't entirely his fault. He was simply playing by unspoken rules that had been set up before he even joined the league. He played in a system that actually rewards rough play, and he thought it would someday earn him a spot on an NHL roster.

Just a couple of nights before Kugel's ridiculous display, in a televised game between the Toronto Maple Leafs and the Buffalo Sabres, Tie Domi of the Leafs and Rob Ray of the Sabres, both better known for their fighting ability than for their finesse, had a set-to early in the game. Soon after, they had a second go at each other. Both of their bouts took place before the 15-minute mark of the first period!

The two enforcers earned over $2 million US between them last year. That kind of income is quite an incentive for Kugel and others whose hockey skills may not be at a high enough standard to make it to the NHL. It's no wonder that Kugel showed that he, too, could play that same style of hockey only a few nights later.

Kugel's ban from junior hockey has since been lifted and he will be allowed to play organized hockey once again. During his time away from the game, he worked with younger players, speaking about fair play, and took an anger management course. It's likely the league and his team management prompted him to get some help for his temper. It's also very possible that his parents took a dim view of what took place and gave him some good parental advice by pushing him to get help for his attitude problem, or at least I hope so. I'm sure Jeff Kugel has learned his lesson well and will take the opportunity to redeem himself. He may not be a very skilled player, but his size is a definite asset, particularly if he is able to develop his other talents. That may be his only chance. Fortunately, the NHL seems to be decreasing the number of goon types on their draft lists, but they still grab as many big guys who can play as they can.

The Ontario Hockey League clamped down on some of the violence during exhibition games this past season because many players spent most of their time on the ice bent on displaying their tough-guy wares to impress the scouts. The fans didn't enjoy it much and headed for the exits. The league ruled that a team would be fined $500 if their players received a total of five major penalties in a game. The fines increased for each further major penalty in the game — a strong deterrent.

I'm knocking junior hockey here some, but much of the time

I still think it's entertaining for the fans and an affordable way to see a hockey game. Fans get to see prospects who have been selected high in the NHL draft and who are likely to make the pros. And they get to watch future draftees show their stuff. Anybody who got to see under-ager Jason Spezza play for the Brampton Battalion of the Ontario Hockey League would surely have been impressed. He wasn't even draftable into the league at that time because he was only 15. Under-agers can play before draft age only in their hometown at the time. (Over the years many players have relocated to a new "hometown" to be able to play for that team.) Today, he could have been drafted because they've lowered the age. Don Cherry's Mississauga Ice Dogs of the OHL selected him number one overall in the midget draft in 1999. He'll likely be selected first overall in the NHL draft in 2001.

As in any sport, there are always a certain number of players who rise above the level they're at, and Spezza is one of them. He's an enormously talented player, and was before he played for Brampton. Just think how magnificent he will be in the future, if the other players aren't always trying to shut him down.

●

The Canadian Hockey League (CHL) has made some changes in their policies and format that increase the quality of play. For example, in recent years, Canadian junior teams have been able to draft a maximum of two European players per team. The Europeans want to come over so they can get used to the North American style of play. The NHL teams have the opportunity to see their offensive prowess in an NHL-style setting, so the experience enhances the young players' chances of being drafted higher at the amateur draft. (In 1999, four of the top 12 players selected at the NHL draft were Europeans playing in the CHL.) And these players have time to adapt to North American culture instead of trying to juggle the rigours of the NHL and figuring out how we do things.

Still, the adjustment to North American hockey for European juniors can be a difficult one and raises red flags about our game. For example, Anaheim prospect Maxim Balmochnykh left the Quebec Ramparts of the QMJHL during the 1998–99 season, saying he was unhappy with the "American" style of hockey and playing on a smaller ice surface. He felt that his skills were eroding. Balmochnykh's concern about the level of play in North American junior hockey indicates that we might want to take a closer look at our game. Is the decreasing quality of play at the junior level a symptom of the overall fall-off in the quality of the NHL game? Will Europeans soon believe that their skills are eroding at the NHL level?

The junior leagues have made some initiatives to curb the violence and improve the quality of kids' hockey, but not nearly enough. They're still catering to the NHL's wants and needs. It's difficult to blame them for that, because their existence depends on it. The way they handled the Jeff Kugel affair and similar incidents shows that they realize there's a problem.

Let's hope they continue to set a better standard and insist on a more open game, and get away from the scrums and the tough-guy attitudes. They need to stop the takeouts away from the play, so players can get to open ice to receive a pass properly. There is an overabundance of fighting in junior, but this is not what hockey is about at this level. It's about developing good, young hockey players who can play the game with skill and toughness, in an entertaining way, without leaning to fisticuffs at every turn.

As a development league for the NHL, the Canadian Hockey League (CHL), made up of the Western Hockey League (WHL), the Quebec Major Junior Hockey League (QMJHL), and the OHL, still produces a high percentage of NHL players. But at one time, it was thought that the U.S. collegiate ranks would take over as the prime supplier to the NHL, similar to the set-up in the National Basketball Association and the National Football League. In 1978, when players were drafted at 20 years old, there were 73 players drafted from U.S. colleges, more than from any of the individual Canadian junior leagues. But when the league changed over to a 19-year-old draft in 1979, the collegiate contribution to the NHL dropped to almost nothing. In 1979, only 15 players were selected from U.S. colleges.

Occasionally, a gem will come out of American collegiate hockey. Those players usually jump to the NHL when they get noticed, but not always. Anaheim Mighty Duck Paul Kariya, for example, was drafted fourth overall by Anaheim in 1993 from the University of Maine. Even though he was a highly touted player, he stayed in school for one more season and played for the Black Bears, as well as for the Canadian Olympic Team, before joining Anaheim.

Realistically, though, elite players don't choose to go to American colleges just to further their education, but that certainly is factored into the equation. Some who aren't projected to be selected high in the amateur draft choose college over junior because if their pro career doesn't work out, they can still get an education.

In recent years, U.S. colleges have produced mature, experienced players who can step right into the pros. Bill Muckhalt, for example, did just that for the Vancouver Canucks this past season, after four years at the University of Michigan.

Sometimes, a collegiate player doesn't show his true abilities until his fourth year or so, and then he's up for grabs as a free agent. Jason Krog, of the University of New Hampshire, won the Hobey Baker Award as the outstanding U.S. collegiate player of the year and signed a free-agent contract with the New York Islanders at the end of the college season in 1999.

The NHL is drafting some players right out of American high schools, and those players opt for the pros because collegiate hockey wouldn't help them get to the NHL (though they miss out on the education). Those players are more likely to play Canadian junior hockey to improve their skills, or to make the jump immediately into the NHL. Pittsburgh Penguin goalie Tom Barrasso and defenceman Phil Housley of the Calgary Flames are prime examples of players who made that jump successfully.

The Ontario League, for example, offers a first-year midget

draft choice one year of tuition, books, and residency for each year in the league. Second through fifth rounders receive a year of tuition and books for each year in the league; any draft picks after that get one year of tuition for each year in the league. Major junior hockey in Canada does its best to keep these players at home with similar offers. They offer these education pursuits as a viable alternative to the NCAA route.

There has been progress in junior and university hockey recently. But there's always room for improvement.

part 2

you wouldn't believe what I saw on the ice

the goon era 4

I t's amazing how many people say that hockey hasn't been the same since the NHL expanded from the Original Six league to having 12 teams in 1967–68. And I agree with them. As a budding referee, I saw first-hand the decline of NHL play into goon hockey.

Naturally, having to stock twice as many teams with twice as many players meant that the talent was diluted. It's not that there weren't a lot of good hockey players in the minors who were ready to move up. There just weren't 120 of them.

The NHL attempted to prepare for the onslaught of new players by establishing a development league in the midwest called the Central Hockey League (CHL). Each NHL team sponsored one CHL club. The NHL supplied the referees for a number of minor professional leagues, including the American Hockey League and the Western League.

I was refereeing in the CHL at the time. With more players needed in the NHL, there was also a need for more referees and linesmen.

I had been training as a referee in the "I," the International Hockey League. When Carl Voss, the NHL referee-in-chief, called me at the end of the 1963 season and asked me to join the pool of NHL officials, I was in heaven. The idea was that I would gain experience and develop along with others in the minor professional leagues in preparation for the NHL — if I proved myself.

I guess I did because I was refereeing NHL games two seasons before expansion at the end of the Original Six era. I was the only referee from that developing group to be called up at the time.

●

Each minor league had its own style of play. The CHL featured good, fast, solid play, with body checking and good playmaking by eager young pros giving their all to make the big time. There were some very talented players in that league in a wide range of years. The AHL, with teams in cities such as Rochester, Pittsburgh, Providence, Buffalo, Springfield, Quebec, Baltimore, Cleveland, and Hershey, was made up mostly of veterans, with a few younger players sent there to develop. The WHL was a six-team league: San Francisco, Los Angeles, Portland, Seattle,

Vancouver, and Victoria. Again, each team had a sponsorship connection with the NHL. The WHL had a lot of older players, so there was a more laid-back style. It was a slower game, with good playmaking and very little nonsense. Of course, there was the occasional oddball, like Howie Young, who some fans will remember for his NHL antics. He cut quite a path through the WHL. I think the WHL players knew their limitations. I thought they might have an unwritten agreement about some things. For example, when a player was tired, he'd hold the puck against the boards, and the opposing player, also tired, would lean on him and wait for a whistle. I generally cooperated — they were a good bunch of guys.

The CHL was unique. It was a new league, stocked mostly by young players being trained for the NHL, with the odd veteran thrown in for stability. It was a great place for an up and coming referee to earn his stripes.

The CHL included teams in Omaha, St. Paul, Minneapolis, Tulsa, Memphis, and St. Louis. Some of these cities had had IHL teams in the past, so the fans were familiar with the game of hockey, and with me, because I had refereed in those cities at other times. I first got to understand what abuse of a referee was at the professional level in those cities.

It was a good time for me as a referee. I received some excellent training in refereeing a number of quality of games in the three leagues. At the same time I got to know and understand the players and the way they thought, and the way they played the game. It was a major step in preparing me for the move up to the NHL.

Some might have thought that the quality of refereeing would be diluted along with the quality of players when expansion came about. But I think that because they only needed to add a few officials, as compared to a large number of new players, we stood the test. Just as there had been good players in the minors who likely could have played in the NHL if the league had more than six teams, such as Bill White, J.P. Parise, and the Plager brothers, there were several referees at that level, too.

As it turned out, I was one of those referees ready to make the jump. Of all the developing officials, I was the first chosen to move into the NHL to referee, part-time at first, with the rest of my games spread out in the minor pro leagues, and then in 1969 a full schedule.

The quality of hockey was pretty good, although loosely played in the early expansion years, and generally pretty exciting. There were enough good players around to maintain a fairly high quality of play, but there were a lot of players who didn't belong in the league at all. That's where a lot of the trouble started, and where the change in the style of play in the NHL originated.

The Big Bad Bruins, for one, were just beginning to play their style of intimidation hockey. They played on that small ice surface in the old Boston Garden, and they had one of the largest teams in the league. They hit everything in sight. They gained a lot of confidence having a young man by the name of Bobby Orr in the lineup leading the way, and it was around Orr that the Bruins developed into a first-rate tough hockey team. Gerry Cheevers was in goal, Phil Esposito was up front as the league's scoring leader. They had tough Teddy Green on defence and people like Derek Sanderson and Ken Hodge at forward. Orr led the pack, both with his exceptional talent and with his intimidating style of play. Few players would take the risk of body-checking him because they knew that Orr would pay them back later with a big check. They usually didn't have to wait too long! The Bruins set the tone for the game. In Boston, on January 21, 1968, right in the beginning of my career, I had to call match penalties for stick swinging, the first time that had been done in the NHL in years.

In 1972, the World Hockey Association (WHA) started up in direct competition with the NHL. In their search for players for 22 more teams, the WHA raided the NHL and the minor leagues, further diluting the quality of NHL play.

This was the start of the goon era. Before the early 1970s, you rarely heard the word "goon" when talking about hockey. If you played in the NHL you could be tough, but you still had to be able to play. Not any more. Many teams had one or two goons, while others had just about a whole team of less talented players whose main role was to shut down the good players from the opposing teams — interfering, hooking, holding, or anything else it took to stop someone from skating by them. This was the way it was for many of the teams, especially the expansion teams, who just couldn't keep up with the teams featuring fast skaters and slick playmakers.

Many teams began to play an intimidating style. They taunted anyone and everyone into fights. Good, young, skilled hockey players never got the chance to develop to their fullest because they were shut down by this new style of hockey taking place in the NHL.

●

In 1972–73 the Broad Street Bullies, as the Philadelphia Flyers came to be known, were born. They had been doodling along at the bottom of the expanded NHL and decided they'd take the lead in the intimidation game. They did have some talented players, though. By 1973–74, they had goalkeeper Bernie Parent, among the best all-time; Ed Van Impe on defence, whose stick-work scared opponents; Clarkie (Bobby Clarke), the fearless leader, as long as he had the bullies in the lineup to back him up; Bill Barber; and Rick MacLeish, who potted many of the goals. But it was the "lesser lights" on the team who made some average players look like stars. They used every dirty trick in the book to win hockey games. I used to say that they would even intimidate the Zamboni operator in the visiting rink if they could. They would do whatever it took to shut down good hockey players and to make more room for their guys on the ice. On some nights, I'd give the Flyers a dozen penalties, when they probably deserved two dozen! They worked on the law of averages. They knew a referee would only call so much.

I've got to give Fred "The Fog" Shero a lot of the credit for the Flyers accomplishments. I had known Fred in the minor leagues when I first saw him as coach of the St. Paul Saints of the International Hockey League and then as a coach in the Central League. He really came into his own with the Flyers. With

Bobby Clarke as his leader, he skirted the rules of the game and took advantage of a league that had fallen asleep, that didn't pay attention to the quality of play, that let anything and everything go.

In 1975, I refereed a pre-season game between the Flyers and visiting Montreal Canadiens. The Flyers fought from the first drop of the puck and took all kinds of penalties throughout the game. In the final minutes, all hell broke loose. I said, "That's it, it's all over." I called off the rest of the game. I remember Clarence Campbell, the NHL president at the time, saying that it was okay that I called an exhibition game, but not to call a regular season NHL game. Well, I don't know if there has ever been a game called with minutes to go on the clock since that game.

The Broad Street Bullies had a super goalie in Bernie Parent and a defence that made you feel like you were entering a war zone, so even if they were down a player or two they wouldn't hesitate to cross-check somebody across the back and force him to the ice. They didn't worry about the referee calling more penalties when they were already short — they were up for the challenge. They didn't like me refereeing their games, because I tried to call it all. They wanted the referees who would let a lot of that crap go.

When some of the really tough Flyers moved on to other clubs in later years and were forced to be actual hockey players instead of goons, they didn't stick around for long. Dave "The Hammer" Schultz flopped in Los Angeles without his henchmen from the Bullies along. "Big Bird" Don Saleski moved on to the Colorado Rockies and just disappeared. These guys had depended on mob rule when they wore their Flyers' uniform, and they couldn't cut it on their own.

The Flyers won a couple of Stanley Cups with their intimidation techniques, in 1974 and 1975. The other NHL teams took notice and decided that they'd better smarten up and get some intimidators, or goons, or policemen — call them what you will. Without at least one goon, a team couldn't contend in the NHL.

Even the famed Montreal Canadiens dynasty of the 1970s saw the light, adding some beef to their tremendous group of skilled hockey players. They had Guy Lafleur, Yvan Cournoyer, but they also had Cam Connor and Gilles Lupien. All the clubs had to get some goons to protect their good players from being intimidated out of the league. Since these players weren't good enough to intimidate with good checking, they became proficient at clutching and grabbing, hacking, spearing, punching — whatever it took.

Could you blame the Flyers entirely for creating this demon in the game? I don't think so. To some degree, yes, but mostly it was the responsibility of the NHL, namely league president Clarence Campbell and his compatriots of the day at the upper management level, who should have taken action against the bullying tactics of the Bruins, Flyers, and other teams. After all, the NHL executive called the shots.

But the NHL was busy wrestling with the WHA problem. The WHA created a tremendous increase in salaries and caused a lot of legal wrangling. It took their attention away from what was going on on the ice. On-ice play was left to self-destruct.

There was no leadership to keep the game functioning properly, and no one thought about the future of the league. They were busy just trying to stay afloat.

The WHA was a serious threat to the NHL. Not only did salaries escalate, but they signed away some of the NHL's biggest names. The WHA became a true threat to the NHL when the Winnipeg Jets signed the Golden Jet, Bobby Hull, away from the Chicago Blackhawks. Many others followed, lured by the big bucks: Gerry Cheevers, Bernie Parent, Gordie Howe, Derek Sanderson, and J.C. Tremblay.

The quality of the NHL game became secondary to the administrative issues of the day — expansion, adding so many new players at the top levels of the game. The NHL and WHA (some said you shouldn't mention the two in the same breath, but the WHA had some good players) were busy focusing on off-ice concerns.

In the 1980s, the amount of fighting decreased as teams tried to keep up to the high-flying Oilers, and fisticuffs took a back seat, at least for a while.

building on the past — the original six arenas

When the final NHL game was played at Maple Leaf Gardens in Toronto on February 13, 1999, it was also the last game to be played in any of the Original Six arenas. I may have been the last referee to officiate in all those buildings.

The Original Six teams were special in their own right, but we also associated them with their arenas: the old Madison Square Garden in New York; Maple Leaf Gardens in Toronto; the Olympia in Detroit; the Forum in Montreal; Chicago Stadium; and Boston Garden.

In the Original Six era, the fans were so much closer to the ice surface than they are now, and I think it's too bad it's changed, because the real atmosphere of the game doesn't carry into the seating area as well if the seats aren't right on top of the action. Even though it's probably a little safer for the referee and the players that many of the fans are farther away from the ice, there's something missing when the fans are that far removed from the game.

Those places weren't just buildings in which hockey games were played when there wasn't a rock concert or some other event going on. They actually seemed to breathe hockey. You could feel it as soon as you walked in their doors. Each arena had its own personality, which is something none of the newer arenas have established.

Chicago Stadium

In Chicago it was noise, noise, and more noise. It was easily the loudest arena of the Original Six era. The fans would join in with their cheering about halfway through singer Wayne Messmer's rendition of the "Star Spangled Banner," and by the end of it, the cheering would be so loud you wouldn't be able to hear your own voice, or hear yourself whistle for that matter.

Chicago Stadium featured a monster horn that sounded after the Black Hawks scored a goal. It just about deafened you if you were standing at centre ice, because it was mounted under the scoreboard above the ice surface, and facing down. We'd generally wait a couple of minutes until they shut the thing off before facing off after a goal.

Chicago Stadium was also famous for its gigantic pipe organ, which was the largest of its kind in North America. The organist, Al Melgard, used to play "Three Blind Mice" when the referee came onto the ice, until the league made him stop doing that. After that, he'd play a couple notes of the song and go on to something else. We'd come on the ice, he'd play those first couple of notes, and we'd look up and give him a big wave and he always had a laugh over that.

Refereeing in Chicago could be a nightmare because our dressing room was at the same end of the rink as the Blackhawks' room. We'd go off the ice at the same exit, go down the same stairs, where we were a captive audience for abuse from angry management and players. Chicago coach Billy Reay, or general manager Tommy Ivan, the Wirtz brothers, or players such as Bill White, who came right into my dressing room to give his views of my officiating and my ancestry one night — any one of them could follow us down the stairs, yelling at us or kicking our dressing room door. And they did it often.

All the old arenas had little things about them that could make life difficult for a referee. At the end of the Chicago bench in the Stadium there was a big space where the door opened. At most benches, the door opened in front of the bench, with the players sitting close to it. I was up on the boards one time getting out of the way of the play. The players came sliding along and knocked me right into the box. I rather nonchalantly got up and went back to the play, with Billy Reay scowling at me the whole time.

The Blackhawks, who moved to the United Center in 1994,

didn't win any Stanley Cups while I was refereeing at Chicago Stadium, but they had some of the all-time great players during my time, including Bobby Hull, Stan Mikita, and Glenn Hall.

The streets outside of Chicago Stadium weren't considered very safe, but inside, the fans were usually at least civil. We'd go to our dressing room before a game, lay out our equipment, and then go back out to get a coffee. The same fans bantered good-naturedly back and forth all the time. Down in the alleyways where our dressing room was, if you went past that hall and under the seats, you'd see all kinds of rats in that area. The rats even showed up on TV. I used to see a lot of cats around that building.

A lot of the arenas were friendly like that, at least before the game. They weren't usually as unruly as the fans in Philadelphia. Chicago fans didn't like Bruce Hood, but that was okay because I didn't like them either, so we were even.

The Olympia

The greatest hockey atmosphere, in my opinion, was at the Detroit Olympia, where the Red Wings played up until 1979. Walking around the Olympia I could feel the vibes of all the great hockey that had been played there, by the likes of Gordie Howe, Sid Abel, and Ted Lindsay.

Once again, the location of the dressing room at the Olympia wasn't located in the best spot for the referees. The Red Wings' room was just down the hall from ours, and back when the late Jack Adams was the general manager, he'd be a regular visitor.

One night we had a visitor there who threw me for a loop.

The visitor wasn't from either of the teams on the ice. Art Skov was the referee for the game and I was just sitting in the room when Carl Voss, the referee-in-chief, came in and started asking questions. Skov threw his skate across the room, and I remember thinking that maybe I shouldn't be there. That was my first taste of dealing with bosses in the close confines of a dressing room.

The Olympia also had an odd players' bench set-up that you wouldn't see nowadays. The door on one side of the Wing bench was actually inside the blueline, so the Red Wings had a big advantage, whether getting a defencemen or a forward on the ice quicker when the play was in their zone. The other door was in the centre ice area so they made good use of this set-up.

During my career, the Wings were on a downswing. In 1979, they moved over to Joe Louis Arena, which didn't seem to have a tremendous amount of atmosphere during my time. The building seemed so large and cavernous, and unless you looked hard into the darkness of the seating area, with the seats back a distance from the boards, you weren't sure if there were people up there — nothing like the atmosphere of the good old Olympia! The fans, who are just about the best hockey fans in all hockey, were exuberant, but the Red Wings weren't a good team, so it wasn't very exciting hockey to be officiating.

Maple Leaf Gardens

I found the same kind of environment at Maple Leaf Gardens in Toronto. The Gardens was a strange place to referee a game.

The fans were so polite. They didn't say much about the referee's calls, or yell at the players. It was almost as if there wasn't anybody in the seats a lot of the time. You had to look up into the stands to see if they were awake. It was the quietest building I refereed in. Of course, I was refereeing the Leaf games when the team was pretty lousy — from 1968 until 1984. They sure as heck didn't have or show much during that time. Oh sure, they had spurts when they'd reach the edge of glory, but remember, those were the Ballard times — a dark time in hockey. What the Gardens lacked in noise it more than made up for in atmosphere. It didn't matter if there was even one fan in the building, when you skated around with those players in the warm-up, the feeling was unbelievable.

You see, I grew up just west of Toronto, but Maple Leaf Gardens was far away to us. We listened to the games on the radio or watched them on television. When I was a kid I listened to Foster Hewitt broadcast games on the radio (even he took a slice off me sometimes, later on), and later I watched the games on television. *Hockey Night in Canada* was such a major part of my life, and of so many other kids'. I would go to public skating at eight o'clock and then rush home for the nine o'clock broadcast start (they didn't televise games from the start in those days).

To be part of that part of hockey culture in Canada, and then be the one skating out onto the Maple Leaf Gardens ice on a Saturday night — well, nothing can replace that feeling. Of course once the game started, I forgot all that stuff and just refereed the game as I saw it. Unfortunately, during that time the hockey wasn't all that great. There wasn't much continuity or excitement to the games, which made it tough for a referee. Refs can do a better job in a more intense, fast-paced game. The calls almost made themselves. The Leafs were such a boring team during that time, with their primary skill being clutching and grabbing. I didn't blame the fans for sitting on their hands.

I refereed my first NHL game at Maple Leaf Gardens. What a treat! I got the call to come up from the minors because a couple of the senior referees had suffered some injuries. That was when there were only six teams in the league. It was a regular NHL game for that era — few penalties but no stiff challenges for a rookie referee in his debut. I was thankful for that. (The real challenges would come in later years.) The Leafs beat the Rangers that night 3–0. Some 18 years or so later I refereed my 1,000th game in Toronto at the Gardens, where it all began. I was the first referee to officiate that many games in the NHL. I was honoured in a presentation by Scotty Morrison, director of officiating (and my boss), at centre ice. Some of the arena staff had a big banner made up and had a bunch of people sign it. It's still one of my favourite keepsakes and hangs proudly in my Milton office.

Between those two occasions, my first game and my 1,000th, I experienced some real highs and lows in that building. In one Leaf-Flyer playoff game in 1977, I had to call a tremendous number of penalties. In a Blackhawk-Leaf game in 1983, I suffered through a disputed goal with a player in the crease (usually let go in those days, with no video to go to).

It would have been a lot better for me if the Leafs had been a good team during my time as a referee (especially during the early eighties) because I wouldn't have made such a handy scapegoat and suffered so much abuse. Nobody at the Gardens had any problem blaming everything on the referee. The day after a game we could read about how we had lost the game for the Maple Leafs.

When Punch Imlach was general manager of the Leafs in the late sixties, he was one of the big reasons we formed the Officials' Association. It was because of the abuse he gave us in the press, and because he used us as scapegoats for the poor showings of his team. We banded together and fought back.

One of the more famous altercations in hockey history took place at Maple Leaf Gardens, and I was the referee. On March 7, 1968, Eddie Shack and Larry Zeidel had a stick-swinging duel. Most players didn't wear helmets in those days — maybe you've seen the picture of the scene with the two players sticks' raised and blood streaming down their faces. The roof of the Philadelphia Spectrum, where the Flyers were to play their games, had collapsed and the Flyers had to play their games on the road. Shack and Zeidel went at each other with their sticks, and actually broke them over each other, creating a bloody mess. It was a scary sight. The incident had been provoked by alleged racial taunts about Zeidel, who is Jewish. The league investigated and settled things with a couple of suspensions, but there was no further action taken. Nowadays, the league handles cases of racial abuse more harshly.

The Gardens was special for many people from the days when many of us could only visualize it by the play-by-play of

Foster Hewitt in his broadcast booth high above the ice. I was glued to the radio every Saturday night. My first time on the Gardens' ice was to officiate an OHA junior game. I remember it well, skating in the building that seemed to be larger than all the other places I had skated in put together. What a thrill! Little did I know at the time that I would be back several years later to referee in the NHL. The Gardens was my favourite of all the Original Six rinks. It didn't have the atmosphere of the old Madison Square in New York, nor the Olympia in Detroit, but it sure reeked of hockey history for all the hockey fans in Canada, and we'll always remember it for that.

Boston Garden

Boston Garden had a small ice surface, with small corners that curved in much closer to centre than in the other rinks. Sometimes I felt like a prisoner out there, trying to get out of the way of players' bodies, sticks, and the puck. I felt as if I had nowhere to go.

I think I was knocked down from the boards (after I jumped up on them to get out of the way) in the Boston Garden more than any other Original Six rink. Some fans sat right up against the glass, and others in the balconies seemed to hang almost right out over the edge of the ice surface. It could be pretty intimidating.

Skating out onto that ice surface for a first timer was a thrill, and usually a first-timer would get a break from the fans — they would realize you were a newcomer and would take it easy on you — maybe for a period or so! But after that, they would take no prisoners. On any call that went against their Bruins, you were in for it. I really had to believe in myself in that building to avoid being intimidated.

The smaller ice surface and the narrow corners gave the Bruins a huge advantage over the other teams. Bruins management knew the ins and outs of the Garden and built their teams to take advantage of that. They generally tried to acquire the players who were good muckers in the corners, who played aggressively, and could do a good job of getting possession of the puck in the slanted corners.

The Bruins penalty box was beside their team bench, which meant all they had to do was hop over the boards to change players when a penalty was up. Meanwhile, visiting teams had to skate all the way across the ice. Of course, they changed that eventually to take away the advantage.

At one time, when you left the ice surface to make your way to the dressing room, you would have to go through the corridor, where it seemed hundreds of fans were standing, ready to jeer you.

Harry Sinden, the Bruins' general manager, was far worse than any of the fans, however. He was constantly telling me that I was no good and I was a lousy referee. His favourite trick was to meet a referee as he left the ice and verbally abuse him all the way to the dressing room. He did that in pretty much every rink I remember refereeing a Bruins' game in. What a class act, eh?

Don Cherry, who coached Boston in the Big Bad Bruins era,

was as obnoxious to me as Sinden was. It was quite a team effort. Cherry didn't like my style of refereeing. He didn't like the fact that I called the cheap crap that went on in the game, the kind of stuff he encouraged then and still does on national TV. His famous line was "If Bruce Hood is refereeing a Bruins game, bet on the opposite team." He and Harry were two of my biggest detractors. Thank goodness a lot of other people in the NHL liked my style!

During the early 1970s, the Bruins became a very brash team. They were a good hockey team and were the forerunners to the Broad Street Bullies, with their cocky attitude of "we can do no wrong." They challenged the rules whenever possible. They didn't like the fact that I was in charge, not them. They always told me they liked other referees because they "let them play." Well, I can tell you if all referees "let them play," the games would have been a hell of a lot worse than they were. Thank God there were referees on the ice who would and did call the game as they saw it. They defied the teams that would do whatever they could to win, and later those teams would use the referee as a scapegoat for their shortcomings.

I haven't had the chance to visit the new FleetCenter, where the Bruins play now, but most people I have talked to say that it ain't like the good old Garden. Geez, I'd hope not. That building was going to be taken over by the rats and mice before long. It did have an aura about it, though. I'll never forget the awe I had when going to the Garden on a Sunday afternoon, and seeing the building full of Boston Celtic fans. The other officials and I would usually wander in for the last five minutes to see the most important action of the game, then return at night to referee a Bruins game. The parquet floor would be gone, replaced by a sheet of ice, with another full house in attendance — quite a memorable atmosphere. There were good pubs to go to near the Garden after the game, but that's a story for another day.

I had some classic run-ins there with Bobby Orr, Phil Esposito, Sinden, Cherry, Derek Sanderson, and many others. I have lots of memories of Boston Garden and all the people who made it a great place to be (and not so great).

Montreal Forum

The Montreal Forum was something else. When I first refereed there, Toe Blake was the coach, and he scared the wits out of me. He was such a dominant figure. I felt I really had to be at my best so he wouldn't holler at me. But refereeing at the Forum was very special for many reasons. It reeked of hockey atmosphere, even when empty. I remember being there one summer when they put in a new concrete floor. There was nothing but piles of dirt and trucks covering the floor, but that old building still had that hockey feeling.

League president Clarence Campbell was in the stands a lot in those early days, and that, too, made me nervous, having so much brass on the scene. He was such an authoritative figure that just being in the same room gave me the feeling I had when the superintendent would come to visit my classroom when I was a youngster. The teacher would have us so scared about the superintendent coming that I don't think I drew a breath all the time he was in the classroom. I had that same feeling when Mr. Campbell was in the room. I felt like an underling, and I kept my head down.

My early experience at the Forum was as a standby referee in the Stanley Cup playoffs. I was back-up to such great veteran referees as Art Skov, Bill Friday, and Frank Udvari. I learned a great deal about the game from them. Of course, being on the ice with my idol, Jean Beliveau, was very special for me, as it was for all officials who dealt with this gentleman.

The Forum was a great place to referee. The atmosphere of the building was something to behold. The fans were so knowledgable (except for the fan who hit me in the head with a piece of toe rubber one night to protest one of my calls — I couldn't do much but have a little laugh and enjoy it along with the fans). The Forum faithful didn't get onto the officials that much, as they knew we were an integral part of the game, but if they thought their Canadiens were getting the short end of the stick, they could howl with the best. Every time I had an assignment to do a game in the Forum, I felt especially proud.

Madison Square Garden

The old Madison Square Garden was the place to be on a Sunday night for a hockey game in New York. It was one of those buildings where you felt like the crowd was right on the icc with you. I got one of my first major injuries there, a broken nose, when a deflected point shot hit me right between the eyes. I received some stitches and a couple of black eyes, which made me look like a raccoon for a few days. I stayed farther away from the net for a while after that. The move to the present Garden, which seemed like such a massive building and had such a different structure than the old one, cost New Yorkers some good old atmosphere.

The fans in New York are unlike those anywhere else. It's interesting to look the crowd over (yes, sometimes in a game when it's kind of boring we can do that . . . only fooling!) and see the different types of folks in the stands. They are into the game like no other. They are devoted to their teams. They accept the fact that the Rangers may not do well, but cheer their every move. They drink lots of beer in the stands, but they aren't as rowdy as those at the Boston Garden. They sure do have their own brand of fun. The atmosphere is just different than in other hockey rinks. The Rangers practise outside the city, so for them, every home game is almost like a road game. There's quite a party feeling.

I enjoyed refereeing good games in a building without bringing the wrath of the locals down upon my head, so my choice as favourite rink could change frequently.

The good part about refereeing in the Original Six arenas was that no matter where the game was going to be played, there could always be an element of surprise. I had to be ready to handle just about any situation that might occur. No matter how rude the fans were, how bad the ice might be, what type of facilities the rink had for us to dress in, or whatever the circumstances, none of this mattered — I had to be ready to go out and call it the way I saw it.

The people who worked in the buildings in the Original Six era became part of the arenas' character. The off-ice staff, such as the ushers, the concession workers, the maintenance staff, added to the mystique of the buildings. And they seem to have worked at the arenas forever. Some of them were there before I started and were there after I left, even though I was there for over 20 years. I found that in all the buildings.

Most of the dressing rooms that the referees use now are completely away from the home team and the visiting team, so there isn't any likelihood that any coaches, management, or players will be in that area. In the old days, I'd often meet fans down there who wouldn't hesitate to tell me what they thought of my officiating.

Years ago, the NHL established a head of security for the NHL and each arena, so you'd have a good escort from the ice to the dressing room and from the dressing room to the ice, and in some cases right out of the arena.

In the Olympia you had to go through the crowd to get to the dressing room, which gave the fans a shot at you. There were always some leather-lungs who made it a ritual to harass the referee, especially in the old Boston Garden, where the dressing room was at the same exit as the Bruins' dressing room. We were a pretty good target for the fans up above, and for the coach, if he wanted to hang around for a bit.

We can never turn back the hands of time. We must move on. I wish that all the wonderful devoted hockey fans out there today could step back into one of those old rinks for a game or two, just to see what it was really like. I know they would savour that moment in time forever, just as I do the wonderful memories I have of them.

expansion of consciousness 6

During the 1967–68 season, after the NHL's first major expansion had just taken place, I was in San Francisco to referee an Oakland Seals game for the first time and I got a first-hand look at the hippie scene.

I made my way through the Haight-Ashbury district, an area that had been taken over by the flower children. I talked to some of the panhandlers I saw along the streets. I learned that as many as 12 of them would live in a two-room apartment. Most had dropped out of school, or had left good jobs, because they decided they wanted to go the "freedom" route instead.

This was a whole new attitude toward life. It was an era in

which young people had rejected authority and the enforcement of any rules. Respect for parents, teachers, policemen, bosses, you name it, went right out the window. That included referees, too, of course.

It was like everybody had been reborn into a new life, where long hair became a symbol of that life and gave everyone the freedom to be what they wanted to be. This new attitude, and these new identities, brushed aside the rules that dictated how they should behave.

I witnessed this change in society first-hand in my own home. My children were in their teens then and went through that phase. Both of my boys wore their hair long and dressed a bit differently, and all three were members of a group of young people who hung out at a clubhouse they had put together in Milton. It was their way of seeking their own identity. I also saw many other young people seeking their freedom on the streets of the cities I travelled to around North America. It seemed like everywhere I turned, I saw people like those I had seen in San Francisco, wearing their hair long and different clothing. They wanted to call their own shots in life.

Marijuana was popular in that era too. At least one of my kids tried the stuff. Marijuana was all around me in my travels, but I didn't really pay any attention until it showed up in my own home. I decided to learn more about it and what was going on not only for myself but for all those other parents out there. When I had learned more, I arranged an education night at the local library so parents could come and learn how to deal with this new-found challenge in their lives. I expected we would have about 50 people out for the evening, but almost 500 showed up. The local library hall couldn't handle everybody. They stood in the halls and outside the doorways. I had the Addiction Research Foundation and the local police come out and talk about the drug. I received many letters of appreciation afterwards for taking the initiative of setting up the evening.

In spite of what my kids experienced during these troubled times, all three of them went on to college or university and to good business careers after "doing their own thing." Randy, my oldest, now has his own electrical company and has developed and patented a couple of related products. Kevin's company assists people with their entrepreneurial skills and he has had a lot of success in business on the Internet. My daughter, Marilyn, is a senior administrator at a prominent Canadian university. I think my kids were typical of the youngsters of the sixties. They did their own thing for a while, and then got on with life in the world of learning and responsibility.

This movement in society trickled down to the hockey world as well. Before this change in attitudes occurred, I found that there was a fair amount of respect in hockey, between referees, the players, and the coaches. Oh sure, there was the odd goon, but in general the players used their skills in a much more controlled environment than the way the game was in the late 1960s. They didn't roar across the ice and slam opponents through the boards, or trash talk other players.

As the referee in a game, I needed to be in charge and keep the game in control. My goal was to allow all of the players to have an equal opportunity to play the game to the best of their abilities. That was before the new attitude came about. Then the role of the referee became a tougher job, just as did those of parents, schoolteachers, and the police. Kids challenged any kind of authority. They challenged almost any call I made. They didn't simply whine, as players used to (which was still annoying), but they showed outright disrespect for my decisions, and for me. On the ice and off, people would let the kids have it their way. The game suffered as fewer and fewer calls were made because the referees didn't want to risk confrontation.

The NHL expanded during this time, and there was an influx of inferior players and coaches who did not act in the best interests of hockey. They showed a complete lack of respect for the game, for the people in it. They were products of society at that time. Before, hockey had been a sport where players competed in an exciting, skilful, hard-hitting environment without having to look over their shoulders constantly in fear of being mugged. The only thing stopping them from being great players was their own limitations, not the actual game itself. That changed in 1967 with expansion.

My role changed as well. I was no longer the man who was completely in charge of the games I refereed, no longer providing an opportunity for the skilled players to play. More often than not, I did not feel comfortable in my role as referee because I didn't have that control. In fact, refereeing depressed me. Far too often I didn't call obvious penalties. Goon hockey was taking over.

As a referee in the late 1960s, I took it upon myself to try to change the image of hockey officials. All of my predecessors had been dumped on and castigated. They had taken all kinds of verbal abuse, not only in the hallways, but in our dressing rooms, the media, and anywhere else there was an audience for outraged idiots to shoot their mouths off about the officials.

When I came along, I was expected to fit into this same pattern, and I didn't like it. Any time a coach or a GM felt they had been cheated on a call or that the referee had cost them the game, they thought it gave them the right to spout off. Everyone said that that kind of behaviour went with the territory. That was our job — to be dumped on. The coaches, players, managers, even the owners could take pot shots at us, and we were just to go on with our job and keep our mouths shut. We certainly were never allowed to reply in the same way. What fun that would have been.

But it wasn't in me to keep quiet and not want to do something about this poor treatment of referees. I believed strongly that this attitude toward the referee should change. I was not happy with the situation. I had never been treated that way in sports, or in life, for that matter. Perhaps I was too soft and couldn't stand listening to the barbs that players and coaches would throw our way. But really, I felt it was time that someone stood up for referees.

Those who refereed before me had good quality hockey to officiate. By the time I arrived, in those early years, with expansion and the changing attitude in society, with everyone not giving a damn about authority, it was a tougher road for a referee. My own keenness, desire, and excitement for the job weakened in that environment. But just about everybody I knew, including many of my fellow officials, wondered why I didn't just stay in line, take my pay cheque, and keep my mouth shut. But I felt we needed more respect as officials, and that if we received the respect we were due it would be the beginning of a more positive attitude in the entire game of hockey.

I didn't want hockey's dirty laundry to be washed in public. If a team had a problem with the officiating, I wanted them to handle it in a more professional way through the league office, rather than running off at the mouth in public. This was why in 1969 I went to great lengths to assist Toronto lawyer Joe Kane in forming the officials' association so that we could speak up for ourselves. Unfortunately, the association had a divided front. Some of us were on the league's side, but the huge majority stood up for themselves and wanted to create a better working environment for the referees. We didn't have immediate success, but eventually there was accord. Today, for example, the NHL has in place a severe fine system for abusive behaviour to referees. I take pride in having contributed to that standard being put in place. These standards seem to be working.

In the 1999 NHL playoffs, for example, Philadelphia Flyers' owner Ed Snider blamed referee Terry Gregson for his team's loss to the Toronto Maple Leafs. Gregson called a penalty with three minutes remaining in the game, and Toronto scored on the power play to clinch the series. Snider and Flyers coach Roger Neilson were all over Gregson and the league, blaming everyone but themselves for the loss. Even Flyer forward John LeClair, who had drawn the penalty, got into the act. The Flyers didn't bother to mention that Philadelphia managed to score a total of three goals in their four losses to the Leafs. They had only themselves to blame for that. The NHL eventually fined Snider $50,000, Neilson $25,000, and Keith Jones, who had entered the melee, $1,000. I think the fines should have been 10 times higher than that.

However, in my day, Snider would have received much more ink for his comments, and people would have listened to him, adding to the environment of disrespect for the officials. The fines would have been considerably less, if they were even handed out. It went with the territory. These were high-stakes games, and everyone thought it was okay to vent their frustrations on the officials.

In one game I refereed at the Spectrum in Philadelphia, Snider ran down to the boards during a game and shook his fist at me over the glass because I had given the captain of his team a misconduct. Heaven forbid that I send Bobby Clarke off the ice in his own building. Clarke was doing his usual trick, circling a few feet away from me and making caustic comments about the quality of my officiating. The crowd would think he was a little choirboy, and Clarke, knowing he wasn't going to get me to change the call I had just made, was working on getting me to make the next call in his favour.

I didn't like the way Clarke acted one bit, just as I was not fond of his habit of jabbing the back of an opposing player's legs with the point of the blade of his stick, among other infractions. But it was just another element of the goon hockey era.

There certainly wasn't much love for me in Philadelphia, the City of Brotherly Love, for the penalties I did call. Fans carried signs and T-shirts recognizing my officiating skills whenever I came to town. Usually my name was featured either before or after a four-letter word. The feeling was mutual.

I didn't always call every penalty, even when I saw them right in front of me. Why not? Well, after a while it didn't seem to matter what I did. The league seemed to want to let the games go with few penalties. They enjoyed the publicity they received for the rough play from the Broad Street Bullies and the Big Bad Bruins. When I called a lot of penalties, tried to keep the game in check, I was the most unpopular person on the ice.

a striped **7**
history

In the Canada-Soviet series of 1972, the Russians embarrassed Canada on their own small ice surface, winning two, losing one, and tying one. At the time, Canada was trying to show that it deserved its throne as king of hockey, but we had to hack and whack our way to overcoming the pesky Soviets.

Bobby Clarke slashed the ankle of Soviet hero Valeri Kharlamov in game six and put him out of commission. It was much easier skating for the Canadian squad after that. Our rough, hacking methods played a large part in getting us back into the series and in allowing Paul Henderson to score his famous goal.

Yes, we won that series, but our game lost some of its integrity. We came to have less respect for the game and for the people involved in it. No one was really in charge, so almost everything and anything was okay. This attitude filtered down throughout all levels of hockey. Young players emulated their role models at the pro level. Soon the kids were thinking that running people through the boards, high sticking them in front of the net, and using all kind of dirty tactics was cool.

One thing that always bothered me when I refereed were the scrums that followed a stoppage in play. After the whistle, players would continue to push and shove. That behaviour creeps back into the game now and then, but now the referee can cut it out by throwing a couple of players into the penalty box, or even threaten to, to eliminate this chaos and straighten out their thinking. I mostly had a cease-and-desist attitude. I'd say, "Cool it, you guys. Get out of here or somebody's going to the penalty box." Usually that worked, but if some still wanted to continue with the nonsense, I would choose the most obnoxious player from each team and send them to the penalty box to let everybody know that I wasn't going to condone unnecessary bad conduct. It wasn't hard picking out the two most irritating players because each team had those who always pushed it to the limit. Sometimes I'd send off two from one team, or I'd choose only one player and give the other team a man advantage.

I also didn't like it when, after a stoppage in play following a penalty call, a player would follow me to the penalty box to debate the call. That stopped when they introduced an unsportsmanlike conduct penalty for that kind of behaviour.

After that, few players risked bugging me as I skated to the scorekeeper's box for fear I might give them a penalty. I didn't have to call those kinds of unsportsmanlike penalties after that — I think I might have called two of those penalties in all the time the penalty was available to me during my career, but the players knew I was mean enough to call it at any time.

The anything-goes era eventually gave way to a different kind of game in the 1980s, a wide-open game, where Wayne Gretzky and his Edmonton Oilers ruled. Teams were forced to loosen up and freewheel rather than play tight-checking, defensive hockey. The goons lost some of their shine. Games ended with scores of 8–5 instead of 2–1, and the hockey was more exciting. It was some of the best and most entertaining hockey I've ever seen. The Oilers won the Stanley Cup in only their fifth season in the NHL by defeating the dynastic New York Islanders.

I always enjoyed refereeing Islander games because they came to play each and every night without my having to put up with a lot of BS. Coach Al Arbour was a treat to deal with. He was a great coach, and had the respect of the players and the officials. He was a vocal coach. At times he had his foot up on the boards giving me his views on a call I had probably missed, but we respected each other. When opposing teams acted up, Arbour would sic Clark Gillies on them to keep them on the straight and narrow. The Islander management had put together an excellent hockey team, featuring the likes of super-centre Bryan Trottier; all-star defenceman Denis Potvin, who checked as hard as anyone, sometimes with a "heavy" stick; the unbelievable Mike Bossy, who could score from any angle; and the one and only Billy Smith in net. People still talk about Smith's antics. He'd slash opposing players' ankles if they got near his crease. He always had lots of room to see the puck. Milton resident John Tonelli helped the Islanders to win those Cups. His work ethic epitomized the Islander style. John played hockey on my driveway with my sons in his developing years. The garage door had many dings in it from his shots!

The Oilers took over from the Islanders. The Oilers' style was more open. They skated more compared to the more controlled methods of the Islanders. Smooth-skating Paul Coffey was the wheelhorse on that Oiler defence. Gretzky was the leader, along with Mark Messier and Glenn Anderson. The team also featured some Europeans — Jari Kurri, Esa Tikkanen, and Reijo Ruotsalainen. The Oilers played exciting, fun-to-watch, and yes, fun-to-referee hockey.

The Oilers changed the way the game was played. Teams had to change their styles and find more skilled players to outfit their teams. The quality of play moved up a few notches for a while, before the defensive style took over.

Now, in the 1990s, the attitude is defence, defence, defence. Set up the trap, shut down the lanes, and so on. The offensive part of the game has slowed to a halt. I retired at the end of the 1984 season, while the game was still fairly wide open, though a lot of fighting still found its way into the game. Most teams still felt they needed goons around because the other guy did. The games I refereed at the end of my career didn't have nearly the amount of unnecessary play that plagues today's game. Oh sure, we had our share of the clutch and grabbers, and the hackers, and coaches who tried all kinds of tricks, but nothing like the planned mayhem that takes place these days, with many of the coaches and assistants working overtime to develop a shutdown style. Hockey suffered further when the league expanded a few times in the nineties. More and more teams simply shut down the opposition, waiting for the odd chance to score, instead of pressing all the time.

The referees are directed by the league to call the game as the league wants it to be called. They have no choice but to do as the league says. It's too bad that the refs don't receive adequate guidance and support to improve the quality of play. Instead, they are hung out to dry as the reason why the quality of today's game is poor. Sometimes the fans are right, though. A call can stop the flow of a good game, but it's likely made to cut down on the nonsense.

Sometimes I even wish that when I was a referee I could have been allowed to spout off like the players, coaches, managers, and owners did. I would have loved the opportunity to give my view of a situation. I still think that in many cases, it would clear up a lot of problems if the referee was given the opportunity to explain what happened on the ice, especially since they're on the ice only feet away from the players. The chance to be able to explain their call on a certain play isn't likely to happen, but I wonder why they couldn't be given the opportunity to say their piece since everybody else is.

The referee could even be given the opportunity to explain how they might have erred on a call. (Yes, referees can make mistakes.) The referee is out there to do an honest, forthright job based on what he observes, no more, no less. But of course they can make mistakes. But too many errors in judgment and a referee will be on the sidelines quickly.

Wrongful interpretation of the rules by the referee, however, is inexcusable. I didn't say *application* of the rules, because as we all know the referee has wide latitude to make his calls, depending on each one's comfort level with his judgment. As long as their calls fall within certain guidelines, they're okay.

●

In 1999, I took part in another media event. It was like old times. I was going to "work" a Stanley Cup playoff game between the Toronto Maple Leafs and Pittsburgh for *The National* on CBC. I was heading into the studio, and one of the first people I saw on the train said, "Oh no, you're not working the game tonight, are you?!"

Well, it felt good, anyway. It had been some 15 years since I had refereed in the NHL and worked a Stanley Cup playoff game, and I was still getting the same rave reviews. But this time it was slightly different. On this night they were studying the effects of the crowd, whether cheering or jeering had to do with how the officials called the game.

I had a great conversation on the train from Oakville to Toronto with a husband and wife who were going to the Toronto Blue Jays game at the SkyDome. They were great sports fans and were fairly typical in their viewpoints of the people I've talked to. They were of an age to remember the good old days, when you could name all the players on all the teams in the NHL. The couple said they still watch as many games as possible on television, but it isn't the same, so many of the games are boring, and "There are so many teams now!"

At the studio, I met a very ambitious and talented young reporter in Stephanie Jenzer, who was going to watch the game with me and discuss various aspects of the game. We were to discuss the calls, the non-calls, officials reacting to the crowd, that sort of thing, all with a camera trained on us.

Stephanie and I watched the entire game from up on the catwalk alongside the immense press box at the Air Canada Centre, with the camera recording our conversations interspersed with the action shots on the ice and the crowd reactions in the stands. I met several people up there who are now members of the press or team scouts and management who were on the ice when I was a referee. It was neat to share a few laughs with them. I even got to say a brief hello to Ken Dryden, currently the Leaf GM, who appeared pretty uptight about the game that was unfolding on the ice below. It was interesting to spend a few minutes with these guys and hear their thoughts about today's game. Because they are all employed in the hockey world, few were willing to say anything against the product that pays their salary, but generally they thought that the league should do something to open up the game more and reduce the amount of defensive tactics.

The two-referee system was in effect for the game as for all Stanley Cup playoff games. The referees were two veterans who were on staff when I refereed, Don Koharski and Paul Stewart. The two worked well together. Generally what one saw, the other did too, and they obviously agreed not to make some calls. I wondered about some of their non-calls, though. Maybe if there had been only one referee more would have been called. I also wondered with this system whether the intensity was the same as when a ref is out there alone, having the sole responsibility for making the calls.

Once the play happens, though, it's over, just that quick, no second-guessing yourself or getting a second chance. You see it and either call it or you don't. I just think that with the one-man system, you are on the hook to judge the play on your own. You know that there's no one else to make the call but you. In the two-referee system, when it's a close judgment call and you decide not to call it and the other referee does, I think that could bother the referee who decided not to call it. He had his reasons for not calling it, and it can't do much for his confidence to be overruled.

But with the two-referee system, it almost made me think I could still be refereeing, with only half the ice to cover. I'm still in good shape.

There were very few controversies in the particular game I was watching for the CBC, so there wasn't much of a reaction from the crowd for us to comment on. Of course, any time things went in favour of the Leafs, whether call or non-call, the fans would shout their token reaction or groan if play wasn't in the Leafs' favour.

There were several interviews with a variety of people for this feature as well. The CBC interviewed the fans about the reaction of referees to crowd noise. When our piece appeared on

CBC national news telecasts a few nights later, I was surprised to see that they didn't use much of my stuff. Apparently I wasn't controversial enough and didn't say what they wanted to hear, that the fans do affect the outcome of calls.

I couldn't give them that, because it just isn't true. It's been proven again and again. A ref will more than likely ignore the fans. When a player whines, do you think the referee gives him a break?

A whining player often doesn't even realize he is jeopardizing himself and his club. Mostly, their pleas fall on deaf ears. I'm reminded of Phil Esposito, when he played for the Boston Bruins in the 1970s. He only said what would give him an edge, and his team came second. If his actions caused the old Boston Garden fans to rant and rave at the referee, all the better. Never once did he offset his caustic actions and words with a positive comment. No way, that wasn't the macho thing to do, and besides, his boss, Harry Sinden, wouldn't have allowed such a thing. Keep the refs in their place, as underlings!

But things have changed for the refs. Now there is only a number on their sweater to identify them, whereas in my day our names were emblazoned across the back of our jerseys. I was the last referee to wear number 1 on my sweater, and then the league used our names instead. We had asked to use our names instead of numbers to help give the officials more of an identity. They reverted to numbers under the new management headed up by commissioner Gary Bettman a few years ago to eliminate the identity of the officials as individuals so that they could focus on the game.

Many fewer negative comments are made about referees in today's game. The NHL has gagged team personnel from the players all the way to top management. They aren't allowed to speak out against the officials, or anything else detrimental to the league. When I was refereeing, it was normal to have your name splashed across the papers and on radio and television as the culprit who caused a team to lose.

This was one of the main reasons I helped form the Officials' Association — to stop teams from washing their dirty laundry in public, and from using officials as an excuse for losing. We threatened to counteract all comments about us with our own about their coaching methods. Wow, did this get their fur up! Heaven forbid that we would be allowed to question a coach's choice of players on the power play, for instance, or other acts that we thought were dumb.

On the ice when a player had made a comment about the way I was calling the game, I liked to tell him that I was going to observe him and make comments about his play. When that player would make a pass that went astray, for example, we could skate by and say, "Nice pass." That would anger him, but he usually shut up after that.

It was interesting that a CBC request to have a shot of me saying hello to the referees coming off the ice and entering their dressing room was denied. "Absolutely not" was the word from an NHL representative. He gave me the wonderful, warm reception that I have become accustomed to by league person-nel over the years. He not only didn't address me directly, despite the fact I was the only one there at the time, but he didn't even look at me as he made his statement, and then abruptly turned and walked away.

You can bet if a player made that same request, his attitude would have been different, even if the request was still denied. It showed me how little importance and respect he and the league placed in those people who are and were responsible for running the actual game on the ice.

It reminded me of the past president of the NHL, John Ziegler, when he spoke to me at the Stanley Cup final game in Minnesota in 1991 a few years after I had retired. Some friends and I had flown there in a private jet to take in the game, and I took the guys to the NHL hospitality room. Ziegler came by and I introduced him to my friends. He said, "Interesting to see someone who is suing us enjoying our hospitality," as he turned like a banty rooster, gave his suit jacket an adjustment, and strutted off. I found his comment chilling.

At the time, some of the veterans of the game — players, officials, scouts, coaches, and even some management who later benefitted — were in court trying to get back some of the pension money that the league had funnelled away from us. Eventually the money was declared rightfully ours. It cost the league millions. I should have thanked Ziegler for the recognition, as we dined on their shrimp and booze.

At the Air Canada Centre, we did go down into the hallway and did take a video of refs and the linesmen coming off the ice. As I shook hands with them, I was looking over my shoulder to make sure I wasn't going to be tossed out by the league brass.

Then it got more interesting. The CBC interviewer was going

into the team dressing room to get some quotes on a variety of things and asked if I wanted to come along. It was something I had never done, and never thought of doing actually, but it sounded intriguing.

We waited in the hallway in front of some big silver doors, at the entrance to the inner sanctum. The big doors slowly opened and along with the hordes of reporters and other press people, many with cameras and videos, we marched into the large spacious dressing room of the Leafs.

But there was no one in sight. They had all doffed their equipment and gone to the showers. Then a press relations person ushered out Lonny Bohonos, the newest Leaf who had come in from the Leafs' AHL farm team in St. John's, Newfoundland. He had starred in a couple of recent games. All of the press types converged on him for questioning, almost in mob style. Steve Thomas came out next, and again about 30 microphones were thrust into his face. He reeled back as several microphones actually made contact with his cheek and chin. They asked him a few more questions, and that was enough for me.

As I left, I wondered what had happened to the good old days when the teams dressed in one big room, went into the adjacent showers, and then came back to change into their street clothes in front of their locker where they were readily available to the press.

official business 8

I t was 1978 and I remember travelling to Boston to referee, and fans were shouting to me, "Hood, you're about as popular in Boston as Bucky Dent!" Since I didn't know what they were talking about it was tough to offend me. I had been made to feel not welcome in a lot of rinks around the country before, but this was a new one for me.

I learned finally that their comment had to do with baseball, with a 1978 playoff game that was played at the end of that regular schedule between the New York Yankees and the Boston Red Sox, who had finished the season tied. The winner of the game would be declared the Eastern Division champion and would go on to play for the American League pennant. The losing team, of course, wouldn't be playing anymore baseball that year.

As it turned out, Bucky Dent was a player with the Yankees who apparently hadn't hit a home run all year, and doing so for him would be similar to a goalkeeper scoring a goal in a hockey game. But in that game, Bucky sent one over the fence to score a couple of runs. It was a major factor in the Yankees finishing the Sox off right there in Fenway Park, much to the chagrin of the Red Sox followers. Now I could see why they compared Dent, who had defeated the Red Sox, to me, an unpopular opponent of their beloved Bruins.

Later on I had the opportunity to meet Steve Palermo, a major league umpire for 15 years at that point, who just happened to have been working the game that day in Boston, and while we were sharing sports memories, the Bucky Dent story came up. Palermo told me that he was born and raised in Boston and that his father was a lifetime Red Sox fan. His father was looking forward to the Sox getting into the playoffs and getting a shot at the World Series that year. Well, when Dent came to the plate and hit his memorable shot to left field, it was Steve Palermo who was umpiring down the line, and who ruled the ball fair, making it a home run.

When the game was over, after Steve and his fellow umps left the locker room, he met his father and they headed home in their car. They had driven for 10 or 15 minutes, and his father hadn't said a word. Steve said, "Did you enjoy the game, pop?"

His dad replied, "Couldn't you have called that foul?"

"No way, Dad, it was well inside the playing area."

"I know, but everybody would have thought it would be okay if you had called it out!"

This was just one of the stories I heard in conversations with Steve, and with a couple of officials from other sports, Red Cashien and Paul Mihalak, when we were in New York taping a pilot for a proposed TV series called *Officially Speaking* earlier in 1999. I represented the hockey refs, with my 21 years of experience in the NHL. Steve, as I've mentioned, had 15 years as an umpire in the American League. Red was well known as one of the top referees in the National Football League (NFL) for 25 years. Paul had been a National Basketball Association (NBA) referee for 28 years.

This was a great group for sharing stories, with about 90 years combined experience in the big leagues. The taping was a lot of fun. We each did feature items, and sat around simply chatting, sharing thoughts and viewpoints about situations that have occurred and do occur in sports.

The show was to be an inside look for sports fans at what goes on behind the scenes and on the field/court/diamond/rink, and to explain the development of rules and their interpretation. I know I learned a great deal about the other sports and the various ways things are handled in their backyard, and it made me realize how much we could share with sports fans of the world.

Also, it was great to have the opportunity to discuss the pros and cons of the various applications in the games. For example, comparing the two-referee system in hockey to the three-referee system in basketball. And on the football field, finding out the various responsibilities of the officials — I had always thought that there were too many of them out there. In baseball, I found out there was much more to umpiring than just knowing the strike zone. Umps have to learn the parameters and how they are applied and how the personalities of the people fit into the mix. Or in basketball, the task that Paul had dealing with seven-foot giants on a very limited space, and being the guy in charge, though he is much smaller than the players.

What I found really interesting is the similarity between our sports in actions and body language. Only the rules are different.

Naturally, if we had to deal with only the rules there would be far fewer problems. But we were dealing with personalities, too. It's always been my contention that on every team there are a whole bunch of good guys, about 10 percent are great guys, and another 10 percent are jerks. The other officials agreed with my math.

I like Red's theory about the yapping coach, for example. He said he didn't mind coaches speaking up because he knew what the outcome would be because he was in charge. He officiated in over 500 pro games, a couple of Super Bowls, a Pro Bowl, and 18 playoff games during his career. His job was to go out there assuming he was going to make the right call and not to be concerned about screwing up. "This is my field, I love being here, and I'm glad these two teams have shown up to play football." What a beautiful attitude.

Red feels the role of the referee is to assist the quarterback in being his best by making the right calls to protect him in his territory. He never lost sight of the fact that the players were only playing a game, that they are human beings just like him, and he didn't hesitate to say "Good throw," or "Great play." He earned many an appreciative glance from players for his friendliness. He had a wonderful viewpoint towards refereeing. I would love to have Red referee any game that I played in, with his inspiring attitude.

Paul Mihalak is another regular guy, a nice guy you enjoy talking with. His life became basketball, and basketball became his life, though he didn't quite plan it that way. He lives in Erie, Pennsylvania, about halfway between Buffalo and Cleveland. As a young man, he refereed basketball around Erie. One night he got a call to officiate in a basketball camp in Buffalo, to fill in for an official who couldn't make it. Paul was spotted there and recommended to the NBA for a tryout, and the next thing he knew he was refereeing in that same league. He lasted all those years — over 2,200 games and four All-Star games — through the many, many changes in the sport. Heck, he had never even seen a big-league game, had never been in a big, professional arena before they let him run the game!

When I asked Paul about refereeing the big guys, he said he just never thought about it, it was all part of the game. But he did say that when he would see the players in street clothes later, he would think to himself, "Geez, those guys are big, and little me is in charge of them on the basketball court. Wow!"

Steve Palermo had always wanted to be an umpire. He had good judgment, good rapport, and was well liked by the players for his demeanor. We talked about his favourite and least favourite managers. The favourite was easy — the guy who would win 100 games in a season. Billy Martin and Earl Weaver were two managers he liked to talk about. "Billy was okay. If he knew he couldn't intimidate you, he would respect you and leave you alone, but he sure could stir things up! Earl Weaver was another story. He didn't respect anybody and was a real R.A. [red ass] almost all the time."

Steve told the story of one game in which he was umpiring, and he called a pitch that was two inches outside the strike zone a ball. The catcher said, "That looked like a strike." So the next time the catcher was at bat, a pitch was thrown two inches outside the plate again, and Steve called it a strike.

The catcher commented, "That looked outside to me."

Steve replied, "Now you've got the idea!"

Palermo's career was cut short in July 1991 when he was shot in the back while attempting to stop a robbery attempt. If not for that, he'd likely still be an umpire today. He was one of the most respected umpires in baseball.

Sport is made up of athletes trying to be the very best they can be, and it is the officials' role to make the playing surface as level as possible, to apply the rules in a way to allow equal opportunity for all players. The fundamentals are the same for all officials in every sport. Officials are the third team on the playing surface. They all have the same desire as the players — to excel at what they do best.

Like the players, officials aren't perfect, either. We talked about screwing up and throwing the wrong player out of a scuffle just to get on with the game, or about being at the wrong end of the field to start the game. And in one instance a particular referee (I won't tell you who) said to a player, "I've got a penalty on your team for tripping, but I've forgotten the number, so I've chosen you to go into the penalty box. I suggest you do and it will be best for both of us."

Critics usually say that you can tell when an official is doing his job because you don't notice him. Anything controversial, of course, and the best you can ever do is have 50 percent of the participants agree with you.

But the officials are closest to the action, have the best vantage point in the house, so of course we're going to notice things that others with a biased viewpoint might not.

Whether in hockey, basketball, baseball, or football, officials are in the middle of the action, and watch their respective sports evolve over time. Some of my views on hockey mirror the other officials' observations of their sports. They can see how the athletes' attitudes are changing, and how the media, salaries, and other aspects of sport are changing the on-field action.

breaking our fighting spirit 9

n *Calling the Shots*, I wrote, in reference to fighting in the game of hockey, "Many GMs, coaches, and players have been quoted in past years in support of banning fighting from hockey. What is it going to take to get everybody on-side?"

Well, it has been over 10 years since I wrote that, and though there is evidence that fighting is becoming less and less a part of our game, it is still around. And I still believe that fighting acts as a deterrent to many skilled young hockey players who want to continue to develop their talents so they might some-day play in the NHL.

Oh sure, the naysayers, the macho types, will all say, "Take fighting out of hockey and you'll see more stick work." That might be true, but slashing, cross-checking, and other illegal uses of the stick can be halted very easily, especially now that there are two referees on the ice instead of just one. Eliminating fighting at the expense of increased stick action is a good tradeoff because the stick work can be cut down, with the right guidance and support from the league officials. Maintaining a firm level of command to continue a standard set from the start of a season through the playoffs takes good leadership and support.

Then there are those who say that if you don't allow fighting, running the goalie will just get worse. Well folks, there are a couple of other people on the ice who can eliminate actions such as that — the referees. All the league has to do is agree on the standard that will apply when a player deliberately makes any contact with the goalkeeper, and the referee will have the power to punish those who run the goalie.

In hockey's early days, fights took place when two players had a disagreement about something that happened between them. They would push and shove each other until finally the gloves would come off and they would go at it. Altercations were as likely to take place between the star players as between anyone else.

In the Original Six days of the NHL, the competition was very keen. Teams met each other 14 times during a season. Often, teams would play back-to-back games — for example, Chicago in Toronto on a Saturday night and the same two teams right back in Chicago the next night. That created plenty of carry-over animosity from game to game, but usually only between a few of the players, who would remember what had been done to them.

In those early days, while the referee looked on, the two players fighting would be separated on the ice by the linesmen when it was decided the players had had enough and would be easy to subdue. The players would pick up their sticks and gloves and head to the penalty box, where they would sit right beside each other because there was only the one penalty box. The odd time they would continue the battle in the box but in those early days that was rare. Usually if it looked like there would be further trouble, a guy would sit in the box between them. In some buildings, a policeman would sit between them, but he wasn't needed that often, and generally he was just there with a great seat to enjoy the game. Think about it: Wouldn't it be nice to have seat right at centre ice, get paid for being there, and now and then get to rub shoulders with some of the greats of the game in the penalty box? Not often though — it was more likely one of the lesser players who entered that area.

Later on, a person was assigned to sit between players from opposing teams every time two players went into the box — not an enjoyable task, at the best of times. Soon, the league came to its senses and assigned each team its very own sin bin. I'm sure everyone reading this has seen more than half a team jammed into one of these small areas meant for about four people at the most.

The game began to change in the late sixties and early seventies with the changing attitudes and major expansion. There was more fighting, and the old-time feeling of the game began to disappear. The players were even ordered not to pick up their gloves and sticks but to proceed directly to the penalty box. If they didn't, they were given an extra penalty.

The NHL didn't worry as much in its earlier days that other players would join in a fight, or a player would come off the bench to join in, but that started to happen, too. That's when they added the "third man in" rule, a penalty for joining a fight, as well as penalties for leaving the bench during an altercation. In 1971–72 they started giving game misconducts to the third man in. The league could see at the time that teams were using bullying tactics, and were fighting in the name of team togetherness. Really, the extra players were out there to bash the other team.

The third man in became quite a difficult rule to call for referees because there were so many variables. Just about every week a different situation would occur, and the league would dictate how we were to handle it. For example, on occasion two fights would take place at the same time and a different player entered each of those fights. Just picture this situation as a referee for a second. You have blown the whistle to stop play because a couple of players have dropped their gloves and are going at it. It's the referee's job to have seen the whole play leading up to such an altercation. (Usually referees do see everything, but not all the time. Sometimes they have to rely on their linesmen to fill them in on some details they might have missed, or they guess who did what, if they know that one player was more of a jerk. More often than not, you'd give out equal time in penalties if you weren't sure.) All the players on the ice are grabbing hold of each other and dancing around while the main combatants go at it. We say the "main" combatants because often the dancing partners on the fringe get into it. Now you have two separate fights taking place at the same time. So when it comes to applying the "first man to enter an altercation" rule, you have to decide if the rule applies to only the first player to enter the altercation, leaving all the others free because they weren't first to enter. Did you throw both of them out the game? In the case of a single fight taking place, if a fourth player entered a fight, would the fourth also be subject to eviction? There were so many different scenarios and the rulings kept changing. The teams had a hard time figuring out how the penalties would be dished out. Many times the officials did, too.

These types of interpretations of the true intent of the rule by those who didn't have a feel for the on-ice game caused referees a lot of grief. And the rules would constantly change according to who argued the strongest about a certain rule. The referees' input was seldom sought, and in fact denied, when offered. We dangled on the end of a string, waiting for the next memo from management to tell how it was going to be, at least for the next game or two.

In the Original Six days, players had great passion for the game, and they played hockey and went through life committed to what they believed was right. This passion could lead to sticky situations.

I remember hearing about one story that illustrates how intense the game used to be. Rocket Richard, the Montreal

Canadien great from the 1950s, showed up at a sports banquet in the off-season as a guest speaker. When he arrived, he spotted NHL referee Frank Udvari and refused to stay for the banquet or to speak. Richard said he didn't like Udvari during the season and didn't like him at dinner either, and that's why he was leaving.

Richard brought a lot of passion to the game of hockey. I think that this kind of passion often made many skilled players, driven to excel at the sport, occasionally erupt into fisticuffs. They wanted to score goals and win hockey games, but that same drive could make them throw off their gloves once in a while, too. Rivalries developed between star players, who would remember their last run-in with a player and keep that in mind they next time they faced off against each other.

In time, fights were no longer personal battles between skilled hockey players. The players only wanted to play the game, and to win. But the fans and the press wanted to see more of the physical side of the game, more fights. The fans and media made more of fighting than the players did. Newspapers ran headlines that said so-and-so was going to get so-and-so during a game. The players' personal agendas became public business. Fights became less spontaneous and seemed to occur at the fans' prompting.

With more fighting came uneven battles between players. Bigger players would go after the smaller players, and it became the responsibility of bigger teammates to step in and come to their rescue. This created a whole new component of the game. Fights were no longer personal but occurred between players who were simply doing their job, protecting their highly skilled teammates.

This attitude gained strength and carried on into the 1970s, the goon era of hockey, when it became inevitable that all teams would have to carry a goon or two (or several in the case of the Philadelphia Flyers). Often it seemed that the whole team was content to exercise mass thuggery to win a game. Even though many of these teams featured very talented players, such as Bobby Clarke and Bill Barber on the Flyers and Bobby Orr and Johnny Bucyk on the Bruins, goon tactics propelled teams to Stanley Cup championships. The style of hockey in that new era crept up on us, and nobody did anything about it. Soon, the thugs flourished, with the Broad Street Bullies at the top rung on that ladder. This style was insulting to the way the game of hockey was intended to be played. Thank goodness, the goon era finally ended, though teams still generally employ at least one tough guy.

Usually when a team dominates the league, the other teams try to find a way to beat them at their own game. I saw this first-hand at an exhibition game I worked at the start of the 1975–76 season in Philadelphia between the Flyers and the Montreal Canadiens after the Flyers had just won their second Stanley Cup in a row.

The teams had played in Montreal the night before, and Canadiens coach Scotty Bowman was upset that the Flyers had pushed his team around in that game. Bowman wanted his guys to stand up and be counted from that point on. They did just that on that September night in Philly. From the drop of the puck, the players fought from one side of the rink to the other. The Flyers' Bobby Clarke (the choirboy, remember) got into a skirmish with pesky Doug Risebrough of the Canadiens, which touched off another full-scale brawl. It got so ridiculous that with only minutes to go in the game, I called it a day and sent all the players to their dressing rooms — game over!

Over the years, I could sometimes see a reason for fighting. Players simply got mixed up in the heat of the battle. But when teams added goons to the rosters to protect their star players, it changed the game forever. The Montreal Canadiens, for example, added John Ferguson to watch out for Jean Beliveau. Fergie was plenty tough and took on all comers, and he could actually play the game. But still his main role was to protect the Canadiens players instead of using his gifts.

Teams would have to stock up on tough guys to keep pace with the other teams, creating a domino effect. In the end, the tough guys were really on the ice to do battle with each other, and the star players could only watch from the sidelines. It became just a show for the fans. The league had sunk to new depths. The mentality of the game had changed. Coaches would no longer simply sketch out offensive plays for their star players, but would figure out how to best match their goons against those on the other team.

I believe that we will see less and less of goons and intimidation tactics in hockey in the future. The NHL has had some success in cutting down the value of fighting to a team by instituting higher consequences, but the tight defensive style that plagues today's game is actually helping to cut down on the number of fighting infractions.

The role of fighting during the playoffs in particular is diminishing. The enforcers just don't get to play very much in the playoffs because teams can't afford to allow them to take dumb penalties, especially with the instigator penalty now on the books. Also, in the playoffs, the benches are shortened. The fourth line, on which the enforcers almost always find themselves, doesn't get on the ice as much.

And now because a smaller percentage of teams make the playoffs, regular-season games have become far more important than they were even just a few years ago. The playoff system used to be ridiculous — 16 of 21 teams made it to the post-season, so the regular season was more or less meaningless for most teams. Now, 16 teams still make the playoffs, but 28 teams are fighting for those spots. I think that because of the increased importance of the regular-season games, the regular season will be closer to the playoffs in style of play, and the goons won't get on the ice as much. That will be a welcome change. In recent years there have been fewer and fewer fights, 20 percent less in 1998–99 than there were in 1997–98.

During my refereeing career in the NHL the number of fights escalated right from the drop of the puck for the 1967–68 season, the year of expansion, until my retirement in 1984. The average number of fights a game peaked in the 1987–88 season.

We had a few ways to curb the amount of fighting. We could give penalties — minors, misconducts, game misconducts —

anything to get the troublemakers out of the game. Later, the league punished the instigator of a fight with a minor penalty.

Does the instigator penalty have an effect on the amount of fighting that takes place one way or another? It's hard to tell. Disbelievers think that the threat of the instigator penalty allows for too much nonsense to take place without any retaliation — too much stick work and interference. The players are concerned about taking the extra minor penalty for being the instigator and don't want to put their team in the hole. I don't agree with that view, especially when you see the number of dumb penalties that players already take at other times in the game that are far more prejudicial to their team. At least if they take an instigator minor, they usually have accomplished something in the form of a message to the opposing team.

That's not to say that I'm in favour of fighting, I'm not. But for goodness sake, don't eliminate the instigator penalty. I think we should go back to giving a 10-minute misconduct for fighting, meaning that a player goes off the ice for 10 minutes, but his team isn't a man down for that length of time. The team isn't really affected by the fight, and besides, they probably don't need that instigator on the ice anyway.

Any number of penalties won't eliminate the spontaneous outbreak between two equal and willing combatants as a part of the flow of the game. I'm not sanctioning fighting, but sometimes people get heated and feel they need to let off steam. Still, they should try to contain themselves, just as the rest of society does. Wouldn't it be neat, for instance, if we could fight whenever we want? We could fight the guy who cuts us off on the highway, or the guy who jumps ahead of us in line at the beer store. That guy would be deemed the instigator, which would make it okay for us to punch him in the face. That's just how silly fighting seems to me.

Teams are now realizing that, yes, they need tough guys, but those tough guys have to be able to play the game as well. A goon who can play the game is twice as good as your average goon. NHL teams can't afford salaries for a team of players who can't skate or score, so big players who can score and provide an intimidating presence are at a premium.

Enforcers earn millions of dollars a season. A big young tough guy who can skate, maybe not even that well, but can fight even better can survive in the NHL at a healthy salary. Why wouldn't our young players emulate these guys, especially when they know that they're not going to make it on talent alone? At least four NHL players, including Tie Domi and Bob Probert, well known for their fists, earned over a million (one player made $1.7 million!) last season. Others earned well up into six figures. The average salary for the top 30 pugilists in the NHL was almost $650,000 in 1999, using information compiled by *The Hockey News*. The average number of penalty minutes these players take during the regular season is in the 200-minute range, and they score an average of four goals in that same time. Seems like a waste of their time and ours, doesn't it?

Today's players are in much better shape than they were a few decades back, and they're bigger. Reggie Fleming, a penalty leader of the Chicago Blackhawks and New York Rangers in the 1960s, would duke it out with another player and would barely be able to breathe after it was all over. He'd happily take his five minutes in the penalty box just to get a chance to get a rest. Fleming wasn't much of a fighter, but I found it interesting to listen to him talk as the linesmen would separate him and the other player. In his raspy voice he would shout taunts at his opponent with what little breath he had left.

The average size of an NHL player has increased dramatically in recent years. It used to be that players of average height could star in the league or rank as a good defenceman. Take the Toronto Maple Leafs defence of 1958–59. Tim Horton was 5'10", 180 pounds; Bob Baun was 5'9", 175 pounds; Carl Brewer was 5'10", 180 pounds; and Allan Stanley, tall at 6'2", weighed only 190 pounds. On that same team, Frank Mahovlich, who always seemed taller than everyone else, was only six feet tall. Even in the 1960s, at 6'2", 196 pounds, I was taller than almost all the players and heavier than the majority.

In today's NHL, if you're not six feet tall and at least 200 pounds, you're considered a small player. In fact, there are only a handful of players in the NHL who play defence and aren't six feet.

Take a look at this list. There are only 11 NHL regulars under six feet tall:

- Phil Housley 5'10"
- Don Sweeney 5'10"
- Lyle Odelein 5'10"
- Mathieu Schneider 5'10"
- Ray Bourque 5'11"
- Alexei Zhitnik 5'11"
- Steve Duchesne 5'11"
- Brian Leetch 5'11"
- Darius Kasparaitis 5'11"
- Dmitri Yuskevich 5'11"
- Calle Johansson 5'11"

The biggest players in the league are:

- Chris McAllister 6'7"
- Hal Gill 6'7"
- Zdeno Chara 6'9"

The NHL, now filled with bigger, tougher, stronger players who are better conditioned and more agile, is threatening to the smaller players and makes for some spectacular bouts. But really, when everybody is so strong and knows how to fight, they don't seem to want to get into it. Fighting just isn't worth it to many of these players.

Those who support fighting in hockey say that there's no problem — nobody ever gets hurt in a fight. I can tell you, folks, not only was that not true when I was a referee, it's even less true today. How could these behemoths not get hurt when they pound each other into the ice? Just ask Nick Kypreos, who last played with the Toronto Maple Leafs, if people don't get hurt. In an exhibition game on September 17, 1997, at Madison Square Garden, in a meaningless fight with Ryan Vandenbussche, he fell to the ice and hit his head after being dazed by a punch. It was horrible to watch what happened after he fell. Blood oozed out of his face. He was out of it, but pathetically still tried to raise his head off the ice. That was the end of his hockey career.

From time to time, you see polls that indicate the majority of hockey fans want fighting to remain a part of the game. Those fans don't really have a reason for wanting fighting to be part of the game. Whether they admit it or not, those people just like to watch a fight. Let's face it, if they allowed fighting in basketball, football, or baseball, people would soon vote against taking it out of those sports, too. And they seem to get along fine without it.

Because people enjoy fighting, does that mean it's a good thing, that it's a necessary evil? Because 16,000 people stand up and yell when there's a fight, and cheer on players like Tie Domi, does that make the game better? No, of course not. When you come right down to it, I think that people just think they want fighting. I often compare the situation to a group of business people sitting around a huge table in a boardroom holding a very important meeting. Suddenly out on the street below, a two-car collision takes place. The people in the meeting hear the shrieking of tires on pavement followed by the abrupt sound of a crash. How many seconds do you think it would take before everybody in the room was at the window gawking? It's human nature, yes, but certainly not for all of us — there are many who just enjoy the good things in life and don't have a need for that added shot of adrenaline that comes from watching a fight.

If the rules against fighting are improved and applied properly and consistently by the referees, the number of fights should continue to diminish in the NHL. The less that hockey has a need for goons, the less work there will be for them. I don't think fighting will ever completely be abolished. Too many people who have influence in the decision-making process think it should remain a part of the game. They speak the loudest.

But fighting is not an integral part of the game. After all, nobody seems to miss it in the playoffs or the Olympics or World Cup, do they? Nobody would miss it in the NHL, either.

What gets lost in this ongoing debate about fighting in the NHL is the bad image of professional hockey it conjures in the minds of the youngsters growing up today. Why would kids want to strive to become professional hockey players when they know they'll have the crap beaten out of them before thousands of people in the stands and a million more on television? How inspiring is that? Oh sure, some kids look forward to participating in an NHL where goons rule because they think that fighting is the only tool they have. That's wrong.

What's even more wrong is that we lose out when the young people who would otherwise enjoy playing the game and have talent might just say to heck with it and play another sport that doesn't allow fighting. No other sport condones fighting as the game of hockey does, so they can choose any other sport they wish!

No one ever seems to pick up on this. I can guarantee you that there are a lot youngsters who lose heart when faced with the rough stuff and drop out, or maybe don't even get involved to start with. There are those out there who will say, "Oh well, if they don't have the courage to play the game, they should stay home." Those people miss the point every time.

What's good about hockey is the action, skills, prowess, excitement, the opportunities the game offers young people, and the anticipation of a game. Notice that fighting is not on that list.

rules are made to be changed 10

I t's funny looking back at television clips of hockey in the 1960s and 1970s: players without helmets, goalies without masks, no curved sticks. It's a reminder of just how much the game of hockey has changed in the last 30 years.

And as the game itself changes, so do its rules. At one time, in those very first days, the rule book was about two pages long. That was when they played on a sheet of ice with no markings, had two 30-minute periods, and forward passing wasn't allowed. A team had to continually move the puck forward, like in rugby. There were seven players on the ice at one time, whereas today there are six.

The rules didn't allow the goalie to fall on the puck, but that changed during the NHL's first season, in 1917. Only three teams even played the first full season of the league (the Montreal Wanderers' arena burned down just four games into the season).

In 1910–11 the NHA changed from having two 30-minute periods to having three 20-minute periods and dropped the seventh player in 1911–12. And in 1921–22, minor penalties were reduced from three minutes to two.

At first, the ice was wide open. Later, they painted two lines, each 20 feet from the centre of the ice, creating three zones. With this change, forward passing was allowed for the first time, but in the centre ice area only.

The rules continued to change in those early days as they attempted to create more offence by opening up the game. More offence? Well, some things never change, do they?

In 1925–26, when the puck had left the defensive zone, only two defensive players were allowed to remain in that zone. This was done to force players to move the puck forward. A team would actually be penalized if a player was ragging the puck, skating around with it so no others could get it. (You wouldn't have to worry too much about players ragging the puck today. Some good stickhandling would be nice to see, but unfortunately the way the rules are applied, it seems almost anything is allowed to inhibit a player from doing just that.)

In 1927–28, forward passing in a team's own end zone and in the centre ice area was permitted. In 1928–29, you could pass into the attacking zone as long as a teammate hadn't entered the zone yet, thus creating the offside rule. Oh yes, you would also be penalized for passing the puck back from another zone into your own end.

Confused about all these rule changes? Well, that's another thing that never changes.

In 1941–42, the NHL went to the one referee, two linesmen system, from the two referee system that had been in effect for many years, and they stayed with this change for the next 57 years, until 1998–99, when two referees were used in several games. The linesmen became able to call more than just line calls, but not when judgment was involved. That was left to one man, the referee. They only wanted one person to be held responsible for calls.

Along the way, they were forced to make a lot of minor adjustments in the game, mostly to close the door on something either a coach or a player had devised to get around a rule. For example, Carl Brewer, while playing for the Leafs in 1960–61, would cut the palms out of his glove so he could grab an opponent without the referee seeing him. Fred Shero, when he was coach of the Philadelphia Flyers, would have his goalie fake an injury or pretend he had an equipment problem to get his team a breather. A rule went in the book to deal with this. The goalie couldn't go to the bench during play to get his equipment fixed. Even if he broke his stick, someone would have to bring a new one to him. Roger Neilson, who has coached many teams in the league with his unique style, most recently with the Flyers, could always find a loophole in the rules. (It's too bad they wouldn't let the refs blast Roger in the press, because they would have gotten an earful!) Shero and Neilson were responsible for a lot of rule changes in hockey. I suppose you could call them innovative, or you could say that they were just good at breaking the rules without getting caught.

Neilson used to have his goalie leave his stick in the crease after he pulled him for an extra attacker, hoping that if the puck was shot at the goal it would hit the stick and not enter the net, so they changed the rule. Now if a goalie leaves the net, he'd better take his stick with him. He would also have his team keep taking penalties in the last two minutes of play to stop the other team from scoring — a team couldn't have less than three players and the goalie on the ice at any one time. The too-many-men-on-the-ice penalties would be delayed. All his team had to do was touch the puck to get a stoppage in play. Another penalty wasn't going to hurt them, anyway. This would upset the opposing team because every time they got the puck they would get hauled down, so there was no way they were going to score. The league changed that rule, calling for a penalty shot against a team deliberately taking a minor penalty in the last two minutes of play. That took care of Neilson's loophole. I bet that if back in 1931 the league hadn't made a rule limiting a team to one goalie in the net at any one time, he would have blocked his net with two goalies.

●

I operated a referee school that brought officials together from all over the world, a group of people who love the game and had a lot of questions. Because of their unique position in the game, referees are able to truly see which rules work and which ones don't. Referees are in an unbiased position, as well, and can see what can be done to improve the game.

When I was a referee, I cared about the game as these referees did. And I'm the type of person who believes something can always be better.

Rule changes often come about from simply noticing a rule is not working. For example, batting the puck to a teammate with your glove used to mean a stoppage in play no matter when it took place, and it was a routine call, almost like an offside call. But then the league noticed that teams would bat the puck to get a stoppage in their own end if the opposing team was applying pressure, especially if the defending player had lost his stick. A player would dive at the puck and knock the puck with his glove to a teammate to get a stoppage in play. The league changed the rule, and players were allowed to glove-pass only in their own zone.

After the advent of curved blades and the varying standards until the half-inch curve was agreed upon, occasionally the ref would be called upon to measure a stick. If a team could prove that a player on the opposing team was using a stick with too much of a curve to it, that player would get a minor penalty. The referee measured not only the curve of the blade but also the width and height of the blade overall because a lot of players would shave it down to almost a point.

Soon we were measuring sticks on a regular basis, which took a lot of time. If a stick was illegal, the offending team would be assessed a minor penalty, and if not, a $100 fine went to the requesting team. This was not much of a deterrent compared to the opportunity to score a goal when the opposing team received a two-minute minor. The rule was changed so that whichever team was in the wrong would get a minor and would have to pay a fine.

Home teams supposedly got into the visiting team's dressing room and would measure all the sticks. They knew when they could get away with asking the ref to measure a player's stick. So further changes had to be made to the rule. In the beginning, the rule was not too clear but the teams were always manoeuvring and challenging every detail, so the strictest of guidelines had to be put in place. The player whose stick was challenged had to be on the ice at the time, not on the bench, among other rules. As I said, the rule book has become quite thick over the years.

Style of Play

The style of play in hockey has changed a great deal over the years, and as the style changes, the rules keep pace. Instead of just sending out lines whenever another line is tired, teams now send out specialty teams in almost all situations. It used to be that when a team would get a penalty, one of the players coming out for the next line change would sit out his turn. Now, there are players assigned specifically to killing penalties. Coaches occasionally school their players in other tactics, like switching up the wing positions, or moving a defenceman up front, to throw the opposing team off its game. The style of a game changes at different times throughout the game. Check, check, check is the name of the game today — shut down any offensive moves by anybody and hope for a break to get a chance to score.

One of the most common techniques used to try to get a scoring opportunity is the dump-in — crossing centre ice and blasting the puck to the opposition end boards and then going in and trying to get it back. It seems dumb doesn't it? You have possession, then you put it up for grabs and try to get it back.

Then there's the trap, which has really slowed the game down in recent years. It's a great defensive tool, but it kills offence. It hurts the game. The league will be forced to deal with it if they want to beef up the scoring stats.

In recent years, in order to avoid stoppages in play, the league adopted the rule that if players were offside when the puck entered the attacking zone, they could put themselves back onside by clearing the zone, which became known as the touch-up offside rule. All of the players had to be outside or touching the blueline together once the puck had entered the offensive zone, then they could go back in. What happened was that teams just blasted the puck into the attacking zone whether their teammates were in the zone or not. When the puck would go back to the defenceman at the point just inside the blueline and it would jump over his stick and go into the neutral zone, he would merely blast it back in and play would continue. Before, a deliberate offside would have been called. But then some teams argued against that rule because it kept them from making plans. So the league went back to the old way again.

Now they are talking about changing back to the tag-up system!

I suggest that they keep the tag-up rule, but don't allow the player putting the puck back in to send it deeper than the goal line, which would eliminate the blast-in. This would encourage more possession by the defencemen. If they put the puck into the zone 20 feet or so, the defending team would be set up to rush it out of the zone. When a player blasts the puck into the opposing zone, it should be ruled intentional and taken all the way down the ice for a face-off in that player's zone. It would encourage more possession and use the entire ice surface and would encourage less dump and chase.

The same goes for icing. First of all, they should do away with touch icing, when an opposing player dumps the puck from his own side of the red line past the other team's goal line, and all a player (other than the goalie) from the zone that the puck had been dumped into has to do is touch the puck to get a whistle. Right now, touch icing only serves to give the networks time to set up for their cutaway to a commercial. It's a dangerous plan, too. Most often, the puck rests along the end boards, so when two players race at full speed just to stop the puck and then have to stop on a dime before they hit the boards, you can see the possibility for injury. A few years back, Al MacInnis, then with the Calgary Flames, was put off balance during a chase to the puck in an icing situation and did the splits when he hit the boards legs-first. That put him out for a while. With the speed of today's game and with the size of the players, an errant follow-through check can injure an unsuspecting player. There's a great risk of head injuries in particular.

When it comes to the start of the game and period, it is very strictly set out that a team will come onto the ice at a certain time and in a certain way and will leave at the end of the period in a certain way. Teams used to take their own sweet time coming out onto the ice at the start of a game, or to start a period. They did this as a stalling tactic to antagonize the opposing team or to protest the officials for a call near the end of the preceding period. Oh sure, there has always been a minor penalty in the book for delaying the game, but it was seldom called. A team would say that no one told them to come back onto the ice, or that their buzzer wasn't working (a buzzer was installed in each dressing room giving a three-minute warning to get ready, then a one-minute warning to come onto the ice). The league didn't deal with this problem properly at the time, probably because the louder voices at the table during talks about rule change prevailed.

This was typical of the rule changes that needed to be addressed when I was a referee. There was so much politicking going on. Usually the heavy hitters or the big voices dominated proceedings and shut down those who came to the table with the best interests at heart, if it didn't fit their thinking. And most of the time they were not interested in changing anything, unless it was going to give their team the advantage.

When players leave the bench during an altercation, the coach is held responsible — he is subject to an automatic 10-game suspension and fines up to $10,000. This is a rule that I vigorously promoted years and years ago. I said there were really only three people responsible for the proper conduct of a game — the referee and the two coaches. And if any one of the three did not do his job properly, the game would suffer. If the coach continually tries to get away with the little things, it affects the game overall.

●

I wrote in *Calling the Shots* about the time I attended an NHL owners meeting with rules on the agenda. I was there representing the officials along with some of my cohorts. We rarely had the opportunity to put our views forward. We weren't welcomed by the likes of the late Harold Ballard, a man criticized for holding back the future of hockey when he was the owner of the Toronto Maple Leafs.

The Leafs went from glory to destruction under Ballard's guidance. Much has been written about his methodology of dismantling the once-proud franchise. Anywhere else in the world, he couldn't have done the things he did and got away with it, but in Maple Leaf hockey-mad Toronto, he survived and did well where it mattered to him — in his pocketbook. It was a shame really — in one of the great hockey cities, this man was allowed to get away with murder. Nobody challenged him. Writers who dared comment in the paper about the poor quality of the Leafs would have their credentials lifted so they couldn't get into the press box. Ballard was a scary, strong individual that his fellow league owners did nothing about. Ballard was a good, if not extreme, example of the types of people who headed up the NHL in the 1970s and early 1980s, people who did not think of the league or the future of hockey, but only of changing the game to their advantage.

Ballard was arrogant and rude at rule sessions. He would sit at the table, holding up and reading the morning papers while the meeting took place. Occasionally, he would blurt out an observation in language more suited for a pool hall.

People like Ballard would shut down those who likely had good intentions of helping the game. I dare say there are types similar to that (I hope not as bigoted) at the table even nowadays. But I think that having a commissioner like Gary Bettman, with more power than the former president position, is a good thing. Bettman can put people like Ballard in their place and not let them dominate the proceedings. I certainly hope so, anyway, in the interests of better hockey.

The changes that have come about in the last couple of years, right or wrong, have come into effect because Bettman has the power to make change. He doesn't have to worry about appeasing the heavies, nor does he have to get a majority vote on everything. And he doesn't have to worry about politics as much as the president would have in the past. "You help me get this change made and I'll help you with yours." I faced that kind of politicking in international hockey years ago. "We'll vote against using this referee, no matter if he is the best and right for the job, in this particular game, if you will do the same for us in an upcoming game against so-and-so." There's no room for that kind of garbage in the NHL.

Whenever we talked about fighting at these sessions, there was never ever any indication by anyone that fighting should be eliminated. Heavens, no. You had to be macho if you wanted to sit around that table. If you talked about eliminating fighting, you faced derision from your peers. If you don't believe me, think about players who have had the courage to speak up against fighting in the league, or about anything else they felt hurt the game, such as clutching and grabbing, slashing, and cross-checking. Mario Lemieux is a good example. He'd be put down by the macho types and would make great headlines on the hockey press beat. The macho attitude kept hockey from looking at fighting for a long time. When Conn Smythe, the original owner of the Toronto Maple Leafs and builder of the famed Maple Leaf Gardens, said, "If you can't beat 'em in the alley, you can't beat 'em on the ice," he meant that you had to be tough enough to stand up and be counted. He didn't intend for the goons to take over.

●

A delay-of-game penalty for holding the puck against the boards was another area that we recommended a penalty for because of delaying the game. Any time there was any pressure by the opposing team, a defenceman would deliberately place a skate against the puck and keep it against the boards, or would "accidentally" fall on the puck to get a stoppage in play. Our recommendation was ignored, however. So instead of making players take penalties for stopping the game, they now hold off on the whistle and make a player holding the puck keep the play moving. This causes scrums in the corners. I'd like to see play kept away from the boards so that the game can open up and the entire surface of the ice can be used. Perhaps allowing only one checker on a player playing the puck along the boards would keep play moving into open ice more.

Also in the past, the goalie would freeze the puck just about any time he wanted to get a stoppage, whether he was being challenged or not. We'd holler at the goalies to put the puck back into play. We would give them a chance, and if they still chose to freeze the puck, too bad — two minutes in the sin bin, served by a teammate who was on the ice at the time. This has discouraged goalies from holding the puck unnecessarily, but some referees are more lenient than others. The goalies know who will let them get away with it.

It seems that almost every rule change, or the application of a rule without actually changing it, was recommended or put forth by the officials long before it was actually changed. I still have records of the suggestions I put forth when I was a referee. I gave my recommendations to director of officials Scotty Morrison, and later to his successor, John McCauley.

On one list from the early 1980s I made 10 suggestions that I believe would make the game better. Eight of the 10 were introduced over the ensuing years. None were directly credited to me, of course. I was just a referee who was there to call the game, not to be involved changing the rules. Still, I have taken satisfaction in seeing my suggestions become realities, even after I had retired. Some of my suggestions: better line designations for fairer face-offs; new rules for players leaving the bench; giving the linesmen more responsibility; and cutting down on the amount of guff officials have to put up with on the ice.

Two seasons ago the NHL asked the American Hockey League to try some proposed rule changes. The AHL has often been a testing ground for the NHL over the years. One experiment that resulted in an NHL rule change was moving the goal line out two feet farther from the back board, which created more space both behind the net and to the sides, creating a different angle of play for all players. It must have taken some getting used to at first. The other rules the AHL experimented with at the NHL's request were ridiculous, but at least they were trying. They tried giving a penalty for stopping behind the net with the puck.

More effort than ever before is being put into trying to fix rules that don't work and to make rules to improve the quality of play. The league has to try, even if it means risking making mistakes. Sometimes the league moves too fast and makes big mistakes, as with the video replay rule for the crease, which created a crisis in the final game of the 1999 playoffs when Brett Hull scored but replays showed his foot was in the crease. Nevertheless, the game is better off for trying.

on a breakaway — the media, salaries, expansion, and agents

11

The on-ice game has certainly changed since my days as an NHL referee. But the off-ice game has changed a lot as well. In the sixties, players first began to fight for what was theirs, and rightly so. But the pendulum may have swung too far the other way. The players now make a lot of money and are influenced by people who may have only a particular player's interests in mind, not the team's, and certainly not hockey's.

The economics of the game have changed tremendously as well. The NHL has discovered a cash bonanza in expansion. In the nineties, they added several teams, with fewer quality players to go around. Now they're considering further expansion, but who knows where they'll find the extra talent.

When we talk about the future of hockey, we show concern for the quality of play and worry about the European invasion, but we should be looking as well at the financial aspects of the game, at who's looking out for whom.

The Media

The media have an interesting attitude about hockey. On one hand, they feel a responsibility to dig up dirt on players or management, not necessarily because they want to but because they are pressured to do so. Their employers demand that they stay one step ahead of the rest of the media.

On the other hand, sports journalists are usually devoted fans of the sport and, just like the players on the ice, have great pride in their work. There are some very astute people in the field who do a great job of bringing us, the fans, the facts in a meaningful and interesting way. Just like on a hockey team, there are media superstars, semi-stars, plumbers, and goons. The latter group isn't interested in discussing a player's background or his idiosyncrasies but would rather dig for smut to make sensational headlines. The media feast on players when they make a mistake, either on the ice or at home. They're like vultures, perched and ready for the players to make a mistake.

It can be difficult for hockey players to perform in a city that has extensive media coverage. They face constant scrutiny at training camp, in exhibition games, practices, game-day skates,

▲ For an official, getting all of the players to sing the right tune is not easy. Sometimes we had to stop a game and rehearse.

▲ Another night of fights in the IHL. It was a great learning experience for me, refereeing in that league. It was my stepping stone to the NHL.

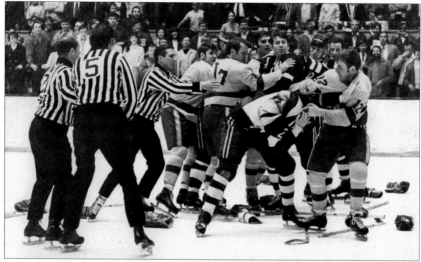

▲ This photo is from an AHL playoff game. There's only one fight taking place, but in those days everybody would join in a scuffle. I'm #5 (I'd moved up from #6 in the "I"). — STEPHEN N. LEMANIS

▲ Bill Barber of the Philadelphia Flyers didn't hesitate to challenge a call I had made on him, so I didn't hesitate to throw him out of the game. Note that I'm wearing #1. I was the last to wear that number in the NHL. — AP

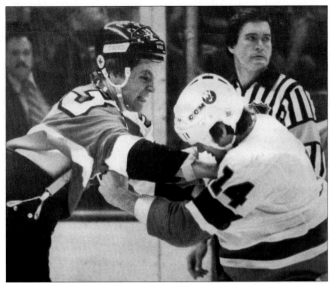

◄

Behn Wilson
of the Flyers,
usually in the
triple digits in
penalty minutes
during his NHL
career, gets
ready to do a
number on
Bob Bourne.

▲ Linesmen Wayne Bonney and Gerard Gauthier do a good job of tying up a couple
of combatants, while I look on to determine the penalties. — HOCKEY HALL OF
FAME

▲ Linesman John D'Amico (left) and I are arm in arm with *Hockey Night in Canada*'s Don "Grapes" Cherry at a fund raising event in Milton, Ontario. I had retired as a referee, and Don as a coach, so he was okay with me being this close.

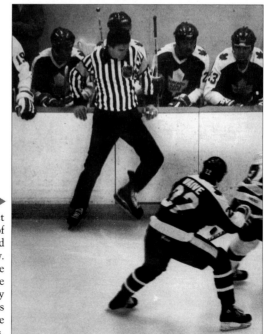

▶
Refs need to get out of the way of pucks, sticks, and players quickly. The boards come in handy quite often, especially at the players bench, where there is no glass.

▲ Former NHLers Billy Harris (top left), Bob Nevin (third from left), me, Bobby Baun (top right), Bill White (front left), Eddie Shack (centre), and Pierre Pilote (front right) enjoy a real beer after finishing a television commercial.

◄

Instructors for the Bruce Hood International School of Refereeing. From the top left, clockwise: Mark Pare, Paul Stewart, me, Bill McCreary, Mark Vines, Gerry Pateman, and Father Jim Armstrong.

▲ The students at the referee school do their morning workout. When I first started officiating, there was little in the way of stretching and preparing the body for skating for a 60-minute game. Later, this training became standard practice.

▲ Look at the intensity of the players at this minor hockey game. Participating in minor hockey is a real treat, especially when the parents voice their support.

▲ Here, I explain to a class at my referee school that it's important to give distinct signals so everyone knows what the call is.

I've worked with the Special Olympics for many years now. I enjoy getting the athletes' autographs. Special Olympians are great sports.

My Old-timer exploits. I played in a tournament in Ayr, Scotland. We had a great time, but the rink was about the size of a large garage. You'll notice the boards are about a foot lower in height than in North American rinks.

We've got the Great One on our side! At a fundraising event in Brantford, Ontario, for the CNIB, at which Wayne was honoured, officials Paul Stewart (left), Ron Asselstine, Andy Van Hellemond, and I managed to get Wayne into an NHL officials jersey.
— *Brantford Expositor*

We, the undersigned honoured members of the Hockey Hall of Fame, offer our support and endorsement of Bruce Hood as a candidate for enrollment in the Hockey Hall of Fame for 1994.

Bruce Hood was the first on-ice official to referee 1,000 N.H.L. games, the first referee selected to travel to the Soviet Union to instruct officials on the N.H.L. system of refereeing, the first N.H.L. referee to officiate in World Championship Hockey, and a founding member of the N.H.L. Officials Association. Bruce designed and created protective referee equipment which is presently used by officials around the world. Bruce Hood refereed 136 Stanley Cup games, and was given the honour of refereeing 3 All-Star Games.

Bruce Hood was a leader in the refereeing profession who performed his duties at the highest possible level of integrity and professionalism. We applaud his outstanding career and we echo Scotty Morrison's June 19, 1984 evaluation that "Bruce completed a most distinguished career and has been a tremendous credit to the National Hockey League."

HONOURED MEMBER	INDUCTION YEAR	HONOURED MEMBER	INDUCTION YEAR
Maurice Richard	1960	Andy Bathgate	1978
Alex Delvecchio	1977	Ted Kennedy	1962
Dave Keon	1986	Bernie Geoffrion	1972
Norm Ullman	1982	Bobby Hull	1983
Pierre Pilote	1975	Dickie Moore	1974
Allan Stanley	1981	"Red" Kelly	1969

◄ Here I am on the speaking circuit, no doubt answering questions from the audience such as, Who was the best player? The fastest? The yappiest? The toughest? and What games were most memorable? I have a lot of fun sharing my memories and opinions with hockey fans.

and of course during the games themselves. The players often do not have a moment to themselves. That pressure on players is much higher in major media centres like New York and Toronto. Players spend nearly every moment of their playing and personal lives on TV and in other media.

In Montreal, the players face the added pressure of having to deal with the English *and* the French press. They suffer more scrutiny than anyone else in professional sports. Every move by anyone in the Montreal Canadiens organization is reported and analyzed — on-ice play, coaching decisions, managerial decisions, any move made by the team president.

I don't believe that the media are simply trying to find fault with the team. But when one media outlet breaks a story of particular merit (few are) and the other members of the press miss out, the media become even more hungry and aggressive the next time they sense a story.

This kind of frenzy is the main reason why teams no longer simply open their dressing room doors to the media like they used to in the good old days. Now, they make players available to be interviewed. Media-player interaction has become extremely businesslike and sophisticated, and much less spontaneous and interesting. In the old days there was more of an understanding, almost an allegiance, between the writers and the sports hero. After all, the athlete was their meal ticket. The writers weren't about to alienate themselves from a player or their team. Nowadays, there is so much press coverage, such a dog-eat-dog attitude, that it is unlikely the old style of personal interaction will ever return.

It's no wonder, then, that many players have developed a thin skin when things aren't going well for them. The pack descends upon them looking for a hot item, or a great quote. The media want the player to blame the coach for playing the wrong line, or they want the player to demand a trade on-camera, or to criticize team management. In recent years, the media have captured several now-famous incidents on film, and the events are talked about for years. I'm sure you remember back in 1995 when goalie Patrick Roy screamed at team president Ronald Corey because coach Mario Tremblay did not take him out of a blowout earlier in the game. The footage of Roy hollering over the boards was played over and over again, and Montreal newspapers ate it up in the following days. The pressure was so intense for the Canadiens that they had to trade their superstar netminder.

Keep in mind, though, that the media have a job to do, and not unlike a player who shadows an opposing player, they're made to prey on individual players. Sportswriters have to pull out all the stops if they want to get the best story available and keep on doing what they get paid to do.

Salaries

One of the major issues in hockey these days is escalating salaries. It seems that every time you pick up a newspaper, there's a story about a player signing a multimillion-dollar, multi-year contract. Even fringe players are feasting in this new era of high salaries. I think the NHL has to take a look at what it's doing or risk losing some of its fan base, which means losing a generation of fans.

The NHL owners have looked at different models from other sports to try to contain salaries. They've looked at a salary cap, and at profit-sharing to help keep the weaker teams afloat. Those are but two of the suggestions that have been put forth in recent years. They may not be ideal solutions, but it's clear that if the owners don't get a handle on the cost of hockey, the game will be in trouble.

I talked earlier in the book about Bobby Clarke and his attitudes about the referee and the tactics he would use during the game. I didn't much appreciate Clarke's on-ice antics, but what I can say about him and other players from the 1970s is that they truly had the will to win. That was the main reason they played the game. Their overriding desire to win at any cost might not have been good for the game, but at least their hearts were in the right place.

The same can't be said for players in today's NHL. It seems to me that what's important to them is how much money they can make. Getting a higher salary has become a big incentive. You don't believe me? Consider that when players are in the last year of their contracts, especially if they are on the verge of becoming unrestricted free agents, they tend to have much better seasons. Why is that? Why aren't they playing at the same level of intensity in the first year of their contracts?

The players are looking after their own interests now, and the team comes second. They don't play through even the slightest injuries any more. I'm surprised at today's players, who can sit out a game with the flu. I can pretty much guarantee that Bobby Clarke never missed a game in his life because he wasn't feeling well.

One respected assistant coach I was talking to in the summer of 1999 told me that he, too, thinks that hockey is nothing like it was in the old days, when it was a fun, competitive game. Now he thinks that the game's all business. Players used to be much more focused during the regular season, he said. Now, only in the playoffs do teams experience team spirit and camaraderie, which used to be such a big part of the regular season attitudes as well.

The players have always received bonus money for winning championships, and for most of them it used to make a big difference in their pay. Nowadays, that financial reward provides little incentive. If a player makes $5 million base salary in a season, what kind of an incentive is a few thousand dollars more? Certainly nothing to knock themselves out over.

Expansion

I think that the NHL will produce a lot of its income from further expansion fees in the near future. The Atlanta Thrashers have been added for the 1999–2000 season. In 2000–2001, Minnesota, which was part of the original expansion in 1967–68 but moved on to Dallas in the mid-'90s, comes back into the fold as the Minnesota Wild. A team in Columbus is being added to the league the same season. The owners are digging for gold in searching out sites for further expansion, but they aren't paying attention to how watered down the NHL talent has become. The quality of hockey was bad enough after the San Jose Sharks, Tampa Bay Lightning, Ottawa Senators, Anaheim Mighty Ducks, Florida Panthers, and the Nashville Predators joined the league in the 1990s. Can you imagine the clutch and grab when 75 or more grinders enter the league? Some of those players will be star players on the worst teams.

I don't understand why the owners are risking a drastic decrease in the quality of hockey. There is a greater interest in the sport now than at any other time. There are many more teams now in the minor professional ranks, and the fans are enjoying themselves. But what will happen if the NHL makes it too expensive for anyone to go to the games?

Minor professional hockey is thriving because fans can afford to go to the games. Many teams in smaller American cities are enjoying great success, with a good fan following. The fans of those teams are showing their loyalty, showing that they truly love hockey. And they're showing the NHL just how much they're willing to pay for it.

In some ways, expansion is a good thing because it creates a large number of jobs for players, executives, and even officials, but it has to stop somewhere. The NHL wants all the money for themselves. They want to be in every market. I don't think they care whether that city can make a go of it or not. They do require a certain number of season tickets to be sold as a condition for franchise status being granted, but after that, the team is on its own.

After the league has exhausted the supply of American cities to expand to, where do they go next? Europe? There appears to be nothing to stop the NHL from becoming a truly global league. There are teams in Carolina and Columbus, so why not add a European division? I'm serious, folks. Expansion to Europe would mean that even more European players would be playing in the top league, which would make for a better quality of hockey overall. I hope, though, that by the time the NHL sets its sights on expansion in other countries, the powers that be in the North American hockey world will begin focusing on skills and fitness over fighting and defensive training.

Agents

During the 1970s, player salaries were not made public. When a player signed a contract, you'd often hear that the terms of the agreement were undisclosed. But the players found that not disclosing how much everybody was making worked against increasing everybody else's salary. It was in the players' best interests as an association, the NHLPA (National Hockey League Players Association), to publish all of the players' salaries. It gave their agents more bargaining power when negotiating for their clients. "Look," they could say, "so-and-so makes this much money, and my guy is way better than him." Agents have driven up the salaries to high levels, but you can't blame them for it. It's their job.

The prevalence of agents has caused another big change in the players' attitudes. The agents work for and are paid by the individual player, so their complete responsibility is to the player. The agents are not necessarily interested in the integrity of the game, and it shows.

I find it interesting that many former players who are now agents, who never commanded big salaries as players, are generating big contracts for today's stars. It's almost as if they hold out for "their guy" to get the almighty dollar they themselves never got, not because they didn't have the talent, but because the system worked against them then. The first big agent, Alan Eagleson, never played in the NHL. In the 1960s, he set the standard for player representation. I wonder if Eagleson had stayed the course in being a player agent, and perhaps had headed up the NHLPA rather than getting "onside" with the owners, how the whole player agent–player salary structure might have developed. The current head of the NHLPA, former lawyer Bob Goodenow from Michigan, led the players on a 10-day strike after a few months on the job. He felt that the owners weren't giving him or the players the respect they deserved. This opened the door for the agents, allowing them to step up their demands for their individual players and become a little more daring at the same time. Imagine how the league would be if Eagleson had stood up for the players 30 years ago.

Some stunts that agents pull damage the league's integrity. And it could work against the agent. In the long run, players may not want to sign with agents who do that kind of thing. And general managers certainly don't want to do business with an agent who has pulled stunts in the past.

Not all agents are like that, of course. Some keep the integrity and the future of the game in mind while still doing their best for the client. They're the ones who suggest that their player not hold out to renegotiate in the middle of a long-term contract. They convince a player not to threaten to go back to Europe if that player doesn't get what he wants. They are more concerned with a player's long-term health than his current money-making value. And they're concerned also with a player's image, which could be damaged by underhanded negotiating tactics. They know how important integrity is both for his endorsement value and in future dealings with teams.

Agents are mixed up in every aspect of hockey now, even going as far as to arrange trades for players, which used to be solely the job of the general manager or team owner. Players used to take their problems directly to the team or to the NHLPA, but now if a player has a problem, he runs to his agent, who is expected to solve it.

On the good side, agents have ensured that players don't fritter away their salaries. They help them to invest their money and set them up for life after hockey. Before, some players who had made poor financial decisions during their playing careers found themselves broke soon after they had retired.

And because agents are concerned with their players' public image, they encourage them to participate in charity events. As far as the fans are concerned, this is the only positive aspect of big salaries — the players giving back to their communities. Many players feel a responsibility to share their time and money to help charitable causes. Let me make it clear that I'm not saying all players help out with charities to further their careers or to relieve themselves of the guilt they might feel for making piles of money. There are a lot of players who help out simply because they want to.

Today's players take a businesslike approach to everything they do. Getting them to participate in assisting with community fund-raising, for example, can be like pulling teeth. They may show up, but, as I witnessed during recent charity golf events, even when the tournament is held in their own hometown, they play golf and then disappear, perhaps so they won't have to give out an autograph without getting paid for it. But certainly they don't have an obligation to be a part of the activities, to give back to the community.

Players from other eras continue to work hard to help out at such events. I only hope that today's players understand that they aren't playing hockey just for themselves. They play for their teammates, for team management, and for the fans. And the kids are watching.

labour relations — get in the game, boys! 12

I n the Original Six days, the owners controlled every aspect of hockey. They were sort of like the parents of the league, and everybody else in hockey was their children.

Most teams were family businesses. The most powerful hockey families were the Wirtz family in Chicago and the Norris family in Detroit. These hockey barons operated their teams like they did their other businesses. The players were employees and had to produce, not unlike factory workers or truck drivers have to produce or risk losing their jobs. The owners thought the players should feel lucky just to have a job in the NHL. They set the work standards and controlled the work setting, and they paid the players what they wanted to.

This is the way it used to be everywhere in the working world, before employees became organized into those dreaded unions and could stand up for their rights. The unions helped to improve working conditions in the factories and mines as well as on the ice, and increased salaries.

Some say that the pendulum has swung too far the other way, that the unions have become too strong and too dominant in the workplace in many areas. You have to wonder, however, what the world would be like now if the workers hadn't organized to create a better working environment with better pay, and what our future would be like now.

It was no different in hockey. The players were like pawns, expected to play the game, keep their mouths shut, and stay in line. If they didn't, they'd go to the minors and never be seen again. More than one player was told this, and backed off and stayed in line. This was the way it was for a long time until the players first got together and organized. Ted Lindsay, then of the Detroit Red Wings, and the Montreal Canadiens' Doug Harvey, two of the top players in the game at the time, started a movement toward the formation of a union — the first National Hockey League Players Association (NHLPA).

It all started back in 1955 innocently enough when Lindsay and Harvey were appointed to represent the players on the NHL Pension Society Board. The board consisted of five members — three league representatives and two players. National Hockey League president Clarence Campbell (the name still makes me shudder), who was in that chair all through the original expansion and the major changes to the league, was there along with an attorney from Toronto and a New York representative.

It was the first time the players had a chance to view what was happening with the players' pension dollars. Lindsay and Harvey constantly asked questions about this and that — the size of the pension, the contribution by the owners, All-Star Game money — but they couldn't get any direct answers.

The teams constantly preached hardship and the financial instability of the Original Six league. All of this was apparently easy enough to do, as they were able to hide their profits in a variety of ways. The most popular method was to report less income and show lower gate attendance. I'm sure this wasn't done to fend off the players, because they didn't think they had to answer to them anyway, but more likely for tax reasons.

The baseball players had formed their union in 1956. The basketball and football player unions had also formed in the same era, so the die was cast for the NHL players to get started. Also, many of the players who were playing in the league at the time had come from small northern Ontario towns where their fathers worked in the mines. They had seen what unions could achieve. This must have had an influence on their decision to form.

Of course, when the league management learned of the formation of the players association in February 1957, they were surprised, and responded angrily. They used all kinds of methods to dissuade the players from forming their association — intimidation, demotion, blacklisting, smearing players in the media (they also controlled the press in the good old days). They would actually trade players — the key union activists — to lesser teams, or demote them, to intimidate other players from joining. In fact, the season after the formation of the union almost one-third of the players had changed rosters, and a tremendous influx of rookies into the NHL occurred.

The team owners had involvement with unions in their other businesses and knew what they could do, how powerful they could become. They weren't about to stand around and let the players have their say. Apparently, it worked. When the next season came along, some players were obligated to sign loyalty pledges to their team. If any refused, they were put on the black-list and would likely be traded away or eventually demoted.

The owners even suggested that some of the players might be communists. (In the late 1950s, many Canadians felt that unions and communism went hand in hand.) Their strategy worked, and it wasn't long before the union was virtually terminated.

The players had threatened to sue, stating that the owners had controlled the hockey scene since 1926 for their own personal benefit, with no consideration for the players. The team owners still refused to acknowledge the association, and with all their tactics, it wasn't long before first one then more players buckled under the pressure. Oh sure, the team officials offered a sweetheart deal — the players could sit on a commit-tee and voice their thoughts — but as for progress of any degree for the players, it all but stopped at that time.

In 1965, it became obvious that a players' association

was inevitable. Conn Smythe, the owner of the Toronto Maple Leafs, was the main leader of the effort to break up the attempted union formation in the 1950s. And it was this same club that under the leadership of one Punch Imlach as general manager/coach, who treated the players poorly, instigated the players to form the NHLPA.

Carl Brewer, a formidable blueline defender for the Leafs, had had run-ins with Imlach over the years and became the catalyst in the early going. He even brought his lawyer to training camp one year, to Imlach's chagrin.

To the owners, hockey was business, big business. They invested a lot of money from their other business worlds into the game of hockey. They controlled everything — the game itself, the players. Many players they owned almost from the time they first started to skate, if they had any ability. The NHL team would sign them to the infamous "C" form, and that player would be the property of that team forever.

Back in 1966, when I was refereeing in the American Hockey League, I refereed an Indians' game in Springfield, Massachusetts. I loved going to cities in the AHL. The people were all so friendly and for the most part, because they were smaller cities, you got to know a lot more people, especially because the linesmen were all local residents. Springfield was among my favourite AHL cities. It had such a small town feel to it.

I learned that there was a lawyer from Canada at the arena to represent the players over a dispute with the team owner. The owner of the Springfield Indians was Eddie Shore, the former Boston Bruin defenceman who made history as a player. But after he became the owner of the AHL team, he became even more famous as somewhat of an autocrat because of his irregular methods of coaching and his general handling of players.

Shore always seemed to have a surplus of players around and had a "players" bench behind the players' bench where the players who were not in uniform to play that night would sit. They were called the Black Aces of the Indians.

This was one of Shore's quirks, just one of many. He would give a player a raise of a few dollars for the upcoming season from what he had earned the year before, because the player had the audacity to suggest he was worth more. A few games into the season, he would fine him that exact amount for "not producing well enough." He tied goalies to the goal posts so that they couldn't flop to the ice on a stop. He had players sweep the seating area, supposedly to help keep the players in condition on their off days. He didn't allow water at the bench. He even got on the microphone during a game and asked, "Is the referee going to call a penalty or not?"

One of his antics I witnessed on a regular basis. As soon as the game was over and the teams had left the ice, he would turn off the ice lights. Gradually, all the lights in the arena would be shut off, so there would only be a few left on in the stands and in the corridors under the seats. By the time we had showered and were leaving the building, there would only be one lightbulb glowing, about 40 watts strong, every 50 feet or so along the darkened alleyway to the door. It was just another way he had to save a few bucks.

This was the man young lawyer Alan Eagleson faced in

settling the need for someone to speak for the players. The players were taking a stand against Shore. They'd had about enough of his antics and the way he treated them.

Eagleson, who had befriended a number of the Toronto Maple Leaf players, among them Bob Pulford, Bobby Baun, and Carl Brewer, had become the agent of the soon-to-be-superstar Bobby Orr. In his dealings with the Boston Bruins on behalf of Orr, he had negotiated an astounding first NHL contract. It set a standard of accomplishment that put Eagleson high on the list as a voice for the players in hockey. This is why the Indians had invited him to Springfield.

Eagleson negotiated an arrangement with Shore, and in so doing laid the foundation for his leadership of all players, and he continued to be a player agent. It was onward and upward from there, with the formation of the players' association soon to follow.

The players accomplished much during Eagleson's reign. For the first time, they had a way of speaking up for their rights. The creation of the players' association and NHL expansion to 12 teams opened the door for players to higher salaries and better working conditions. They negotiated a better pension system, though of course the pension debacle has come back to haunt the NHL in recent years.

The players of that era brought the league to its knees through the courts in the 1990s. They initiated a class action suit on behalf of the former players. They accused the league of using the excess pension monies that the players were entitled to for their own benefit.

The players won the suit. It cost the league millions of dollars to make it right, with hundreds of players, scouts, management, and even referees and linesmen receiving compensation. Carl Brewer was the catalyst, with his prodding to bring available information to the surface. Brewer's former friend, Alan Eagleson, was the person responsible for allowing the league to use the funds by his so-called agreements on behalf of the players.

As for the actual games, it seemed as if they didn't exist as far as the players' association was concerned. The association put little effort in trying to raise the quality of the game, to improve levels and their application, and reducing the amount of goon hockey.

The expansion to 12 teams diluted the product — twice as many players were suddenly playing at the top level. The expansion "success" led to further expansion to 16 NHL teams by 1972–73, with another 12 teams added in 1972 following the formation of the World Hockey Association.

Alan Eagleson was very busy developing a hockey business all on its own — international hockey. The games between Canada and Russia in 1972 began it all. The success of that tournament led to the creation of the Canada Cup. I officiated the first two Canada Cup series. These tournaments turned out to be a good sideline for Eagleson, who required the cooperation of the teams in allowing him to get the players to participate.

The profits from the Canada Cup tournaments were never entirely accounted for, causing Eagleson's eventual downfall. He was convicted of fraud and resigned from the Hockey Hall of Fame.

Many of Eagleson's dealing were not necessarily in the best interests of the players and the game. He capitulated to the wishes of the owners, or, to use a hockey term, stayed on side. That way the players were freed up to play in his prize, the profitable international hockey series.

We will never know how much better the game of hockey could have been had Eagleson had good intentions all along, and truly had the players' interests at heart.

Once again, I think it would have been best for Canadian hockey if we had lost the 1972 series. Eagleson may never have been able to get so close to the players or their money.

There is little doubt in my mind that the NHLPA did nothing to keep the game at a high level of quality of play. Was Eagleson, the unchallenged man at the helm of the NHLPA in those meaningful years, responsible in part for the poor quality of hockey that took place in the 1970s? I certainly think so.

I had gotten to know Alan many years before when he first started to associate with hockey players. I had played some tennis with him at the Orr/Walton Hockey School at Orillia, Ontario (I believe he was instrumental in creating the school, as well as his many other endeavours). I talked with the young players at the Orr/Walton school about a referee's perspective of hockey. My sons attended the school, and they worked there when they were older. I remember the excitement I had in meeting Bobby Orr at the school. At that time he was just in the process of turning pro and entering the NHL, almost at the same time I was. He was a gentleman then and now, though we did have our differences on the ice, on occasion.

Alan was always a happy-go-lucky guy. I admired him as someone who could get things done. I remember going to see him at his office in Toronto when we were in the throes of forming the officials' association. He gave me some good advice that I passed along to Joe Kane, our start-up lawyer who did a marvellous job of getting our NHL Referee and Linesmen Association recognized in 1969. Up until that time we took what we got, without any providing any input. Afterwards we were able to speak up, including having input into the rules of the game and their application — not that we were given much of an audience, because too much of the old school attitude prevailed, and officials were just looked upon as a necessary evils.

An awful lot has changed in the way management has handled players over the years, but the owners still run the show. Oh yes, they receive input from their general managers, but for the most part, a lot of the ideas for rule trials, proposed changes to the game, etc., come from the owners, who often don't have a handle on what is best for the game. Otherwise, how could anyone explain the silly rules the NHL tried out during the 1997–98 season in the American Hockey League, such as going behind the net for a second time with the puck constituting a minor penalty?

I find it interesting that the quality of play on the ice began to deteriorate in the late 1960s and '70s, when the league was busy protecting itself from the players' and officials' associations, trying to outmuscle the WHA, and wrestling with its own problems with expansion. The game itself was secondary more than ever then, so no one spoke up about the poor quality of play that developed — when brawn, intimidation, and fighting took over — and the skilled aspects of the game fell by the wayside.

The other professional sports have taken measures to protect their star players, to disallow illegal or dangerous tactics that put the big-money players at risk. For instance, look at basketball, a game where the "inside stuff" could easily put a star player on the sideline with an injury very quickly. It rarely happens because they have rules both on the court and off to curb dangerous play. Look at professional football. The NFL is constantly worried about how they can protect the quarterback and the downfield receiver. Even in baseball, they have come down very harshly on pitchers who purposely throw a ball at the batter. They can be thrown out of the game.

Our game was allowed to deteriorate because nobody spoke up about it. Fighting is an example. In truth, the players would sooner just play the game than have to put up with the threat that somebody might punch them in the face at any time only to keep them from scoring. But nobody will speak up against it. It's a macho thing. Nobody wants to be branded as a sissy or as someone who can't take it.

A few quality players over the years have spoken up about fighting, as I've already said. Mario Lemieux, one of the best ever to play the game, was called a suck. Well, it's possible that he might have been able to play the game for a few more years had the correct number of restraining fouls being called in the

1980s and 1990s. It's tough to skate and stickhandle when you are carrying a couple of opposing players on your back. If you've ever seen some of the highlights of Lemieux's marvellous goal-scoring prowess, you know what I mean.

●

The formation of the NHLPA back in the 1960s was an absolute necessity in order for the players to get properly indemnified for their efforts as professional hockey players. Up until that time, the owners were making mega bucks for their investment in the sport, while paying the players very little. Within weeks after the formation of the NHLPA, the base salary was increased for an NHL rookie from $7,500 to $10,000 a season. Also, the benefits package and pension plan values were soon increased, and salaries in general started to rise.

In 1972, when the World Hockey Association was formed, another 12 teams vied with the NHL for the top talent, and salaries soared to even greater heights.

The players took advantage of the bidding war that occurred between the NHL and the WHA. This war lasted throughout the 1970s until the NHL cooked a deal with the WHA, which resulted in the dismantling of the WHA, and the addition of four teams to the NHL.

The NHL-WHA merger slowed the increase in salaries for a while, but the NHLPA put on its creative hat and worked on deals with the team owners to recognize the seniority its players were developing. This was the stepping stone to getting free agency for the players and the right to bargain for their salaries based on a number of scenarios, including salary arbitration.

The officials were along for the ride and enjoyed increased salaries across the league. For example, when I retired after the 1983–84 season my salary was $75,000. Today, a referee at that same level receives four times that amount. Not bad, considering the cost of living sure hasn't increased 400% in that time. The linesmen who were underpaid at an even lower rate got a sizable increase to a much better level as well.

Today, the players are in the driver's seat. They really decide what their salaries are going to be and what the working conditions will be like. There doesn't seem to be any end to the skyrocketing salaries. Most players now, even the fringe players, are millionaires.

The pendulum has swung too far in favour of the players. Teams are losing millions of dollars (according to the owners) and it appears that players couldn't care less as long as they get theirs. At one time the players needed an association to protect their rights and to get what they deserved. Now it seems the owners need their own association to fight back.

But if the owners choose to continue paying the players' enormous salaries and can justify it on their bottom line — who can argue with the system? I think, though, that the owners deserve a return on their investment. After all, they're the ones who take the risks in the beginning and pour money into the team. I wonder if Mario Lemieux, the former star player and now owner of the Pittsburgh Penguins (with a group of investors), is planning to lose money?

Spending has gotten out of control and nobody is sure who is at fault. Even Gary Bettman, the commissioner of the NHL, wonders about that. Who is really at fault here? The owners? The players? The agents? I suppose you can say the teams are the victims of a situation that they themselves created and are now suffering the ill winds that blow from it. Will the salaries level off or even decrease to more sensible levels? Well, stay tuned — it's likely to be a long ride before that happens.

Just when the NHL started to talk about escalating salaries, and the smaller market teams cry about not being able to compete with the big market teams, teams like the Rangers, who recently shelled out millions to Theoren Fleury, take salary levels to even greater peaks.

Something is definitely wrong. Team executives now manage their teams according to their budgets, rather than constantly trying to acquire the best talent possible. Smaller market teams are in trouble, especially in Canada. It's survival of the fittest for teams like Edmonton, Calgary, Ottawa, even Montreal.

Part of the problem is that the owners have different personalities than they used to. No one loved Harold Ballard or the Norrises or Marcel Aubut, but at least there was a face behind the team. Now, conglomerates own more teams than individuals do.

I still hear people (the old-timers, of course, me included) who say that it ain't like it used to be when there were just six teams and you knew all the players. Now there are 28 teams, with the addition in 1999 of the Atlanta Thrashers. There are more than 600 players in the league, so being able to know who all of them are is out of the question for all but the most fanatic.

The players rake in a lot of money from the fans, who, believe it or not, know where their money is going. The high salaries they're paying turn off many of the fans, and turn people away from the sport. Look at what happened in baseball. The interest in baseball has never been the same since the 1994 strike and the players' greed was played out in the press. The interest in basketball is not like it used to be, either. NBA players receive exorbitant long-term contracts. It's getting so that a middle-class family can't afford to go to a game — it's far too expensive. Also, most season tickets are held by corporations or by wealthy people who can afford the high cost of going to the games. The higher ticket prices means that fewer kids get to go to NHL games. It's too expensive for them. I think that if kids don't go to see their heroes play live, they may not show the kind of interest in playing like their heroes the way they used to. The NHL can ill afford to lose its young fans, or to diminish the pool of young Canadian players.

Nobody ever speaks up for the fans. Maybe they need to organize an association. If things don't begin to change, and the spiralling ticket prices don't level out, the fans will start watching the games at home instead.

part 3

in love with the game

she shoots, 13
she scores!

Since before the turn of the century, girls have put on skates and played hockey with their brothers on village ponds. In the 1920s and 1930s, women had their own leagues, but by the 1950s and 1960s, hockey was almost completely dominated by men.

A women's hockey team started up at McGill University in the early 1900s under the following conditions:

- There had to be a guard at the dressing room door.
- No boys could watch.

● The players had to be "comfortably and warmly dressed" in long skirts and heavy woollen sweaters.

You sometimes hear NHL coaches commenting that their players look as if they were wearing skirts during a particular game. The women who played early this century actually did. One old picture even shows a woman goalie with a skirt almost completely covering her pads!

I think it's wonderful how the popularity of women's hockey has continued to increase every year since those early days. The women's hockey movement, which was derailed in the 1950s and 1960s, is gaining popularity. The attitude that hockey was not a sport for ladies, that women should be feminine, pretty, and decorative, is thankfully disappearing.

In the late 1970s women's hockey started to come into its own. In Milton, where I sponsor a lot of local kids' sports programs through my business, I was delighted by the opportunity to sponsor one of the first girls' teams put together in the town in 1992. Up until that time I had sponsored only boys' sports.

I met a lady named Abby Hoffman in 1986, two years after I had retired as a referee. Abby had a great deal to do with the change in that attitude, when we became members of the Fair Play in Sport Commission for Canada. I actively participated alongside several business and sports people of pretty high calibre for six years in promoting my interest in making hockey better. The commission had good representation from across Canada in both the sport and business sectors: Murray Costello, then the head of amateur hockey in Canada; Ed Chynoweth, head of the Canadian Major Junior Hockey League; Wayne Gretzky, as the first honorary chairman (followed later by Jean Beliveau); Russ Jackson, the Canadian football great and high school principal; Diane Jones-Konohowski, a former Olympic athlete; Dr. Andrew Pipe of the University of Ottawa's sports medicine clinic (he's now the superb chair of the Committee of Ethics in Sport for Canada, which replaced the Fair Play Commission); Geoff Gowan, the president of the Coaching Association of Canada, whose television commentary on track and field is as good as anyone's; veteran sportswriter George Gross; Ralph Mellanby, former producer of *Hockey Night in Canada*; Tom Nease, former head of Adidas Canada; Gilles Neron, author of the Neron Report on Sport: and Dr. John Pooley, professor at the School of Recreation, Physical and Health Education at Dalhousie University in Halifax. Our objective was to level the playing field in sports for everyone across Canada.

Abby was director-general of Sport Canada at the time. I had heard her name in connection with sports for many, many years. Abby was and is very well known and respected for her distinguished track career. She competed in several Olympics, as well as the British Empire and Pan American Games, but her name meant more to me for another reason.

I remembered reading in the newspaper about how Abby as a young girl played on a boys' hockey team in Toronto in 1956. It was big news at the time and was discussed for weeks. In those days it was unheard of for a girl to be playing boys' hockey. The league hadn't known she was a female when she signed up.

When they found out they booted her out of the league. All she wanted to do was play hockey. Abby was only nine years old at the time. Remember, this was that era when it was not proper for a girl to play hockey at all, much less on a boys' team. Abby's folks went to court and the Ontario Supreme Court ruled against her being allowed to play.

Hoffman was a pioneer in a number of ways because it raised the question of girls playing hockey. Before she made headlines, everybody assumed that girls just didn't want to play organized hockey.

Nowadays, girls are more than welcome in any hockey league. If they want to play with the boys, they can. Many have even graduated to rep hockey, and some even play at the AAA level. If they can prove themselves at tryouts, they can make the team.

Now, just about every community in Canada has girls' and women's hockey. The success of women in hockey reflects a change in society about women participating in sports.

When I ran my referee schools, a few women participated in classes, both in my schools in Canada and the United States. Some of these women planned to referee men's leagues, while others wanted to learn more about the game, its rules, and their application, so they could help to set up women's hockey leagues.

Having women attend the classes was quite an adjustment for everyone, as I recall, not only for the other students, but for the instructors, as well. The instructors were mostly NHL officials, and they'd never had to teach a female how to referee before. It just seemed so different, not for any reason other than they were girls (or young women, I should probably say). They generally were good skaters and understood what my job was as a referee. (I couldn't always say that for the boys/men in attendance. Over the years we had some wonderful young officials who went on to great careers in the NHL, but we also had other memorable students who even after a week of training didn't get it!) Once the instructors adjusted to the new addition to the rosters, they welcomed the opportunity to teach officiating to an entirely new group of people.

The students generally came to the rink dressed in their refereeing workout gear, so there were no problems as far as dressing rooms were concerned, and for the most part, other than that they had their own private rooms at the dorms, they fit in well. They were usually right at the centre of the fun that took place during the school, on and off the ice — all a part of the learning curve of being a good hockey official!

Any time the local press came to cover the schools, they usually wanted to interview the female students. The press, too, thought of women referees in hockey as a unique idea, and so it was at the time. Today, though, there are many competent women hockey referees. There are hockey schools for girls only, so a referee school exclusively for them can't be far behind (or might already exist).

In 1975, the Ontario Women's Hockey Association (OWHA) was formed to organize women's leagues. In 1982, they held the first Canadian National Women's Hockey Championship in Brantford, Ontario, the town Wayne Gretzky made famous. The teams competed for the Abby Hoffman Cup.

Another big name in the world of women's hockey is goaltender Manon Rheaume. She was the first woman to ever play in a major junior hockey game, when she played net for the Trois-Rivières Draveurs on November 26, 1991. She also had tryouts with the Tampa Bay Lightning in 1992 and 1993, and even played for their farm team in Atlanta during the regular season in 1992–93. She deserves a lot of credit for raising the image of women's hockey to a new level, not only for her ability to play the game well, but for the exposure she earned for women's sports. Rheaume played for Canada's national team in the 1998 Olympics.

At a charity game I refereed in Mississauga, Ontario, the mayor of that city, Hazel McCallion, was one of the celebrities in attendance. She had played hockey at one time, and at this game she came onto the ice on her skates and carrying a stick. This was extraordinary because McCallion is a senior. When she stepped onto the ice, she fell down. I thought, *Oh my God, she's broken a hip for sure.* But no, she just jumped up and, in her very spry way, took a couple of turns around the ice to the cheers of the fans. There was no holding this lady back, in politics or on the ice.

In the United States, the NCAA (National Collegiate Athletics Association) officially recognized women's hockey in the early 1990s. The Amateur Hockey Association of the United States (AHAUS) operates a number of leagues, which have greatly expanded in recent years.

Internationally, the International Ice Hockey Federation (IIHF), the governing body of world hockey competition, set up its first Women's World Hockey Championship in Ottawa in 1990. Women's hockey gained international recognition when it joined the Olympics as a full medal sport.

The Canadian and American Olympic teams developed a wonderful rivalry during action at the 1998 Olympics at Nagano, Japan. Fans of both countries were tremendously excited to see their favourite stars battle it out for the gold. Cammi Granato from the U.S. team and Cassie Campbell from Canada became world-famous athletes during the Games. The United States won the Olympic battle, but Canada came right back in 1999 and won the World Championships.

Boys learn how to play hockey almost from birth in Canada, and they're encouraged to play throughout their youth and into adulthood. They even play in seniors' leagues. For them, hockey is a way of life.

For women, however, hockey has only recently become a big part of their lives. In recent years, women's hockey saw its highest participation among older women. Their enthusiasm has trickled down through the system and has inspired young girls to play. Now, girls are becoming excited about the sport as early as boys.

The Halton Twisters Hockey Association, a girls' team that operates near where I live, just finished its third year in operation. The Twisters play in the small communities of Acton and Georgetown. In just its third season, the league had 170 registrants with many more on the waiting list.

When a five-year-old makes a good play, scores a goal, or makes a great save, it doesn't matter if the player is a girl or a boy. It just matters that they're playing the game of hockey and loving it.

The game of ice hockey is just as wonderful for women to play as it for the men. Whether it is a young lady of seven or eight just starting out, or a young lad, there is an equal excitement — all the more reason for us to keep our game as good and clean as possible. Who knows? Someday there may be women playing in the NHL, or in their own pro league. They seem to work harder to develop their skills than do many of their male counterparts. I know I'd sure enjoy watching them play.

same game, different rules
14

You never know what you'll come upon in life. You're going along, and suddenly you run into something that changes the way you think about things. I certainly didn't know how much my involvement with deaf ice hockey would change the way I think about the sport.

My hometown during my NHL career as a ref was Milton, Ontario, which was also the home for the Ontario School for the Deaf, as it was called in those days (it's now known as Ernest C. Drury Regional School for the Hearing Handicapped), where hearing-impaired children came to live and get their education. It was a marvellous institution that Milton was proud to have within the town. It offered employment for locals and provided excellent educational and recreational facilities, including two large gyms and a pool.

The school was also the home of my referee school for many years. It offered fantastic facilities. The people who worked at the school, who cared for the property, took such pride in their work. The quality of the people and the facilities, and the caring small-town atmosphere, made it easy for parents of hearing-impaired children to send their children to a facility that would help them get an education.

I became good friends with the director of the school, Roy Wollaston. We played a lot of tennis. I learned a great deal more about the hearing impaired and what life is like for them. I was proud to be a guest speaker at a graduation dinner in 1983, the first time anyone had to translate my words for a large audience.

One day, I was at the local arena to watch some kids play minor hockey. This group of young lads, who were obviously there to play hockey with their teams, came up to me. One of the young lads pointed to his back, held up two fingers, and then put his hand to his mouth as if to whistle. I wondered what was going on, and then I realized that the kids were students from the school for the deaf. Pointing to my back indicated that I was number two (I wore number 2 on the back of my NHL sweater then), and the blowing of the whistle sign indicated that I was a referee. We became friends in a different way then and there. We always said hello any time we met each other, whether at the rink, on the streets of the town, or on the school grounds.

These boys had been at the arena to play hockey in the local minor hockey system. Obviously the school year enveloped the hockey season, and as these youngsters were in residence at the school for the entire school year, they couldn't play in Wallaceburg, or Petrolia, or whatever other community throughout the province they were from.

Playing hockey wasn't easy for these kids. This was the regular local minor hockey association for the town, and the hearing-impaired kids were placed on teams at their age level, so there was often only one or two on a team of hearing players. At the time, an automatic two-minute timer would buzz, sounding that it was time for the team to change lines. Obviously, they couldn't hear the buzzer, nor could they hear the referee whistle for a stoppage in play. Most of the time they would continue playing after a whistle or the buzzer sounded until they realized that the others had eased up. But they played hard and enjoyed themselves nonetheless, and there were some great lasting friendships created with the local kids.

Later on, through my travel business, I made it a priority to put something back into the surrounding communities. Part of this was becoming involved in hockey for the hearing impaired. I met a gentleman by the name of Roy Hysen from Mississauga, Ontario. Roy, as it turned out, got things rolling for organized hockey for deaf players in Ontario. The first call I got from Roy was on the telephone at my office. I received a call from Bell Canada's TTY/Teletypewriter System, which is available for use by those with hearing, speech, visual, or physical disability. So when the Bell operator informed me she had a call via TTY,

I didn't know what she was talking about. But I soon learned. Roy, who is hearing impaired, is a very persistent and likeable guy, and I became involved in many different ways. Roy was instrumental in developing the Canadian Deaf Ice Hockey Federation (CDIHF), which got started in 1983. The federation was incorporated in 1987, with Roy as president. Paul Pellman, a lawyer from Toronto, was also on the executive. As an attorney, he represented several deaf clients. Jim Rolling of Etobicoke, whose hearing-impaired son was a good young hockey player, made up the balance of the executive. These gentlemen were responsible for a good deal of the fund-raising that kept the federation afloat. I admired their efforts to sponsor hockey in the community.

So when the CDIHF asked me to help them out with fund-raising, I looked forward to doing so in any way I could. Through my travel business, I acted as a sponsor, and I assisted in booking flights to travel to other cities and towns. As a former NHL referee, I became directly involved in the hockey program itself. I refereed some of their games and assisted at their training camps. As a "celebrity," I helped gain recognition for the federation and increased interest in the fund-raising events. A team of hearing-impaired players even played against the NHL Old-timers, which I of course refereed!

In April 1989, millions of Canadian hockey fans eagerly watched Team Canada at the World Championship of Hockey in Stockholm, Sweden. Meanwhile, a small group of hockey fans keenly watched for the results of an International Deaf Hockey Tournament taking place in Voronezh, Russia. Czechoslovakia,

Russia, and Canada fought it out for the medals. The Russian team defeated Canada to win the championship, although our team outshot and outplayed the Russians in the final game.

I had the pleasure of refereeing some of the games in their cold, rather cavernous building. All we had was the common denominator of our love of hockey, which doesn't discriminate. The whole event, my second trip to Russia for a hockey event, was a wonderful experience — the flights to Zurich and on to Moscow, the 10-hour train ride to Voronezh, and the hospitality of the local people. I made the entire trip by myself, as the team had gone on ahead a few days earlier. With no interpreter along, I didn't know which stop to get off at or how to order food in the dining car. It was a challenge for me, but nothing near the challenge the hearing-impaired kids were up against.

The Canadian Hearing Impaired Hockey Association (CHIHA) was formed in the mid-1980s to "develop the interests, attitudes, and skills of young deaf Canadian hockey players, both boys and girls." Jim Kyte, a former first-round pick of the Winnipeg Jets in 1982, was a teacher at the hockey school. In the NHL, Jim made stops in Pittsburgh, Calgary, Ottawa, and San Jose. He left the NHL after the 1995–96 season. Jim was a defenceman, and while he did score on occasion, he mostly contributed with his fists. He was usually into the triple figures in penalty minutes each season, some of which I gave him in the first couple of years of his career. We joked about that when we met at the school. He's a congenial man, popular with the students who work hard under his guidance.

In April 1989, millions of Canadian hockey fans eagerly watched the performance of Team Canada at the World Championship of Hockey taking place in Stockholm, Sweden. Meanwhile, a small group of fans keenly watched for the results of the International Deaf Hockey tournament taking place in Voronezh, Russia. Teams from Czechoslovakia, Russia, and Canada fought for top spot. Russia beat out Canada, though the Canadians outshot and outplayed them in the final game.

I enjoyed participating in hockey schools in Vancouver in 1989 and the following year in Quebec City. I could tell that these schools were developing some good talent for future teams at all levels. They were selecting the best deaf players to participate in the worlds.

Barrie Elliott, a Milton resident and local star hockey player, taught at the School for the Deaf in Milton, and was a teacher at deaf hockey schools across Canada. He was also the first coach of the national team, and was honoured with an award for his contribution. I always enjoyed playing Old-timers hockey against Barrie. He was difficult to check — he wouldn't let me have the puck very often!

I participated in more hockey schools in Vancouver in 1989 and in Quebec City in 1990. I could see the CHIHA was developing some good future hockey players at all levels. Their goal was to have their best players selected to go to world-class tournaments.

In 1991, hockey was played for the first time in the World Winter Games for the Deaf, which took place in Banff, Alberta. Russia, the United States, and Canada fought for the medals.

Canada came away with the bronze. All of the games were tight, well-fought matches, played before sold-out crowds in the arena in Canmore, Alberta. I was glad to have been able to watch some of the action. The U.S. team was coached by two former NHL players, all-star Stan Mikita, who played for the Chicago Blackhawks throughout the 1960s and '70s, and Gene Ubriaco, who toiled with Pittsburgh, Oakland, and Chicago in the late 1960s.

In 1995, now with six countries represented, Canada moved up the ladder, winning the silver medal at Tampere, Finland. Finally, our team captured gold in March 1999 at the tournament, which was hosted by Switzerland in their beautiful city of Davos.

I remember wondering even before I went onto the ice to referee a game of hearing-impaired players how they would know when there was a stoppage in play. They had a fairly simple system in place. Instead of the referee's whistle or the arena's horn, the league uses a series of red lights at both ends of the rink at the top of the boards. When there's a stoppage in play, the lights flash on and off. Even with this system, some of the players with their heads down and barrelling along would continue for a few seconds after play had stopped. But generally the system worked very well.

Members of the deaf sports community consider their athletes to be "part of a cultural and linguistic minority" rather than disabled. They sure showed me how well they could play the game. The success of these hearing-impaired athletes has provided me both with inspiration and a new insight into our game.

●

Another variation of hockey I've had the pleasure of participating in is sledge hockey. The players have permanent functional and/or sensory disability that does not allow them to play regular competitive ice hockey. The players are secured into a seat with straps across their feet, legs, and hips. They project themselves along the ice with 30-inch hockey sticks in each hand. There's a blade on one end of the stick to play the puck and a pick on the other end to help push themselves along.

The sledges, on which the players sit, are narrow devices, about the width of the body. They're about four feet in length and have blades on the bottom to glide along the ice.

I found out just how competitive sledge hockey can be when I was involved in a game for the first time at Maple Leaf Gardens in Toronto in January 1996. A sledge-hockey team put on a demonstration of the sport against the Canadian National Women's Hockey Team between periods of an NHL game. I was the guest referee for the few minutes that the players were on the ice.

It felt strange to be so high above the players. But after I became used to it, I could really see the flow of the game develop as they attempted various plays. The women's team tried their best, but couldn't match the talents of the players who regularly played strapped into those portable chairs.

These young athletes are in very good condition and have the great upper body strength needed to manoeuvre about the ice and to propel the puck. They make passes, just as in regular hockey, and body check as well. They really go at it.

The rules of the sport were first created in 1992 and were rewritten in 1997. The basic rules of hockey are used, but amendments are made according to the circumstances of a particular game. There are three age brackets and also three categories, depending on the degree of impairment of limb usage.

The league places Plexiglas along the boards in front of the player benches so the players can see out onto the ice when they're on the bench. The entrance to the bench is at ice level to allow the sledges to slide right through the door.

The camaraderie of these youngsters is the same as in any game, with lots of cheering for each other on the ice. They love to win, as do we all in any sport, but for them the ability to get out on the ice and play hockey is a big part of their victory. One father I spoke to was so delighted to have found out about sledge hockey. He had grown up playing hockey and was happy to be able to see his son get out onto the ice and enjoy the game as well.

One boy, who was able to play regular hockey, was thrilled when his disabled brother started playing sledge hockey. The brother strapped himself onto a sledge and regularly played hockey with his brother.

The determination and excitement the hearing-impaired and sledge players show in their approach to playing the game of hockey demonstrate to me the kind of spirit that is so important to enjoy the game to its fullest. That goes for the youngest tyke who is taking to the ice for the first time right through to the pros, and on to us Old-timers. For the majority of us, our passion gives us the drive to participate in the game, even if at a slower pace.

the old **15**
skates still fit

They used to call it old-timer's hockey, but in more recent years it's become known as adult hockey, mainly because it isn't just us old-timers who were getting together to play. Adult hockey now includes young adults in their twenties and thirties.

I always find it interesting how many people played hockey when they were kids, and then quit for a while — they went off to school, or got married and raised a family, or established a career. Later on, they take up the game again.

In adult hockey, men and women play in organized leagues. Mainly, they scrimmage and have a lot of fun.

The sports equipment companies realized a few years ago that adult hockey was becoming a big business. They've dedicated lines of hockey gear specifically for this age bracket.

Adult hockey is becoming so popular that communities are fighting for ice time with minor hockey programs, public skating, figure skating, and other kinds of hockey.

I enjoy playing in my Sunday morning league. My league is truly for old-timers — you have to be over 35 years of age or more to play. So what am I doing at 63 playing in this league with these "kids"? Having fun and getting a little exercise. I'm the oldest player in the league, but not by much. So many of the players are in their fifties that we could actually have an over-50 league with the players we've got.

I play shinny with another group on Thursdays during the day, and as if that wasn't enough, I also play on Tuesday nights. Part of the attraction of playing on Tuesday nights is going out for a beer at the Legion afterwards. Mainly, though, I'm thrilled to be able to play with my sons — Randy is 44 and Kevin is 42. How many fathers get the privilege of playing with their sons?

Randy and I play on the same Sunday morning team (sponsored by Bruce Hood Travel, of course), and he brings along his two sons, Alex, who is 10, and 6-year-old Connor, so I get to see them more often, as well. Who knows, maybe some day, three generations of Hood boys will get to play together.

My friend Barny Henderson, a lawyer in Milton, is a typical adult league player. Barny plays two or three times a week during the winter and gets out onto the ski slopes as much as possible. In the summer you can find him playing slow pitch or playing tennis at the local courts. Barny is just a youngster, having turned 50 a couple of years ago.

My barber, Steve Gervais, is a good example of a guy who simply enjoys the game. Steve played all his minor hockey in the Milton community and coached minor hockey for several years, and still plays now at the old-timer level. He was also a highly respected referee in minor hockey for a number of years and still referees some old-timer hockey. He plays summer hockey to get out of the house and to avoid the J.J. (job jar). Steve is one of those people who is devoted to the game. He eats it and breathes it. And he gets to share his views on the game with the captive audiences in his barber chair. I wonder about the depth of his hockey knowledge, though — he's a long-time fan of the Philadelphia Flyers.

On any given night, you can find carpenters, pilots, dentists, lawyers, real estate folks, farmers, salespeople, chiropractors, teachers, you name it, down at your local rink enjoying themselves and getting involved in their community. Professional hockey could learn a lot from these people who play simply for the fun of the game, without the hang-ups of salaries, television contracts, salary arbitration, and expansion.

For many, playing hockey in later years is even more enjoyable than when they played as youngsters. They play just for the fun of it. As kids, they were likely under great pressure to win and had limited ice time to develop their burgeoning talents.

Just as minor and major hockey is organized, so too is adult hockey. The head honcho of one of the largest adult hockey associations, the Canadian Adult Hockey Association, based in Ottawa, was at one time Larry Regan, the former general manager of the Los Angeles Kings. Larry and I got to know each other following a scuffle on the walkway to my dressing room after a game in Oakland, California. Larry wanted to challenge a call I had made in the game and we got physical with each other. After we had both retired from the league, we ran into each other a few times at old-timer events, and had some laughs sharing memories about the old days in pro hockey.

Adult hockey tournaments are taking place across North America and around the world. It's not unusual for teams to plan their vacations around tournaments they participate in in other parts of the world.

Florida was one of the original locations for tournaments and has now become one of the most popular sites for adult hockey tournaments during the winter, for obvious reasons. Even referees go along, since there are few referees living in Florida. One former NHL referee, Ron Wicks, currently a real estate broker in his hometown of Brampton, Ontario, takes some vacation time and referees tournaments in Florida and other warm southern U.S. locations, when he can fit it into his schedule. Ron also enjoys travelling around the country refereeing charity games with his NHL hockey buddies from years past. Often they played against other old-timers in nearby towns to raise funds for charities. They play fun hockey, with a little expertise thrown in.

But you don't have to travel far to become involved in adult hockey. There are so many tournaments in Canada that teams can pretty much take their pick of venues. Many families make a family outing of these tournaments.

Adult hockey even has at least one newspaper to call its own, the *Hockey Old-timers News*. The newspaper, which is published regularly, features many interesting stories of old-timers, including some NHLers, and games of the past. It's also a great source for schedules of tournaments throughout the country.

Many people I speak to at charity events or on golf courses tell me that they once played hockey but haven't played in years. Those who have never played but have always wanted to ask me how they can get involved. I tell them about all the opportunities to play adult hockey out there, and that they should get started or get back into it as soon as they can. You're never too old to learn. They consider my suggestion at least, and I'm always pleased to think that they will have the opportunity to share a love for playing the sport, no matter what age.

Think we love the game of hockey? You betcha!

wayne gretzky — 16
more than just a
hockey player

Wayne Gretzky was good for the game of hockey.

If I had to single out an individual player who has been more instrumental in influencing the game of hockey than anyone else, it would have to be Wayne Gretzky. I doubt many people would disagree with me on that one.

Gretzky has made a wonderful contribution to hockey with his incredible play, his diplomacy, his efforts on the international scene, and the success with which he helped to develop hockey in the United States.

Gretzky was the greatest hockey player ever, on or off the ice.

He was the best ambassador of hockey in our time, and probably for any sport, for that matter. The man had class. He rarely,
if ever, said the wrong things when interviewed. Occasionally,
he might have slipped up, but that's understandable considering
he was the most quoted and most interviewed player in the
history of the sport. For him, it was always the game first,
followed by his team, and then him.

I think Gretzky learned how to be classy from his family. I
got to know the Gretzkys while participating in fund-raising
events in Wayne's hometown of Brantford, Ontario. The events
raised money for the Canadian National Institute for the Blind,
which also makes its home in Brantford. (I know, I know, a
referee, often accused of needing better eyesight, assisting in
fund-raising for the blind. How ironic.) Wayne and I assisted
in tennis, softball, and golf tournaments and gala dinners. His
entire family was involved.

Wayne gives almost all of the credit for his success to his
father, Walter, and I think he learned a lot from his dad. Walter
is something else. I run across him all the time, whether it's at
fund-raising at old-timers' hockey games, a lacrosse series, or
some other charity event. I might have only one argument with
Walter Gretzky. In *Gretzky*, Wayne's autobiography, Wayne
says that Walter once told him, "No matter how good you are,
there's always somebody better." That wasn't exactly true, was
it, Walter?

Nobody has done more for the game than Wayne Gretzky.
That's not to take anything away from Bobby Orr, who also
changed the way the game was played. Before Bobby Orr,

defencemen didn't provide much offence. Orr took absolute control when he was on the ice. He decided how a particular game was going to be played, and he dominated. Gretzky was the same way.

My fondest memory of Orr was the 1970 playoff game when Boston defeated St. Louis in overtime to win the Stanley Cup. You've probably seen the picture, the one of Orr following his game-winning goal, flying through the air with his stick raised in victory. The picture was voted as one of the ten best pictures in sports history. And I'm in it. Well, at least my forearm is. If you look down in the left-hand corner you'll see my hand, wrist, and some striped jersey. That's me.

Both Orr and Gretzky created quite a stir in their early years in minor hockey, setting their leagues on fire with their play-making and unbelievable scoring prowess. Gretzky came to the pros in 1978, at a time when hockey was making more moves toward expansion and the WHA had formed as a rival to the NHL. Wayne started his professional career with Indianapolis in the WHA as a 17-year-old and was sold to Edmonton, where he finished his WHA career. When the NHL added four WHA teams, the Oilers claimed Gretzky as a priority selection, which means they were able to hold onto him.

The greatest player in the history of the NHL was not predicted to be such a success early in his career. They said he was too small, too slow, and a poor skater. Even his success in the WHA — 110 points in 80 games — didn't impress everyone because the WHA wasn't considered on par with the NHL, or even close. Anybody could score in that league, which wasn't all that far from the truth.

But Gretzky wasn't just anybody, of course, and he had no trouble scoring in the NHL, either. Glen Sather, the savvy general manager of the Edmonton Oilers, chose Gretzky as the cornerstone of the Oiler Stanley Cup teams, to create an exciting brand of hockey, never seen before or since. His teams always played a "let's go for it" style, rather than the defensive style that has plagued the game in recent years.

Gretzky's timing was always perfect, even in his first few NHL games. His arrival, during the end of what I call the game's Dark Age when goons ruled, helped take the focus away from the brawling and put it back on the skill of the game. In his first NHL season he won the Hart Trophy as the most valuable player, and the Lady Byng, as the league's most gentlemanly player.

Teams tend to copy the tactics of successful teams. The rest of the NHL copied the Flyers and their bully tactics, until they saw that the Oilers could win a different way. The Oilers scored goals and played an exciting offensive style. They also won four Stanley Cups in five years starting in 1984. When teams saw how Gretzky and the Oilers played the game, the style of play changed throughout the league, making it the highest-scoring era in league history. Of course, teams later devised defensive tactics against that style, and the game was changed again to what we see today.

That's not to say that the Oilers were choirboys. They needed a way to protect their superstar because the rules didn't protect superstars much in those days. Gretzky had Dave Semenko and Marty McSorley to patrol the ice for him, to keep opposing goons at bay. That's why I think that Gretzky never really spoke out against fighting — he could see a need for it in the game, at least at the time. He preferred to play the game by the rules, evidenced by his wall of Lady Byng trophies, but he wasn't the type of guy who would speak out against his team-mates and friends, or their jobs. I believe he just lived with fighting and considered it part of the game.

One of Wayne's claims to fame was setting up in his "office" behind opposing nets. He did that at first to keep himself in the game. He was getting banged up setting up in the slot, which was the style of centres in those days, following on the success of players like Phil Esposito. But Gretzky learned he could do a lot more from behind the net. Of course, he could do plenty in front of the net, too.

The first time I refereed Wayne in a game was in Edmonton. I had of course heard all about this youngster from just down the road from where I lived in Ontario. I remember skating around the ice surface before the game and looking this slender youngster over, and wondering if he really was that good. I thought to myself, *How does he do it?* He was so slight. Then I dropped the puck for opening face-off, and he took control. It was as if he knew what was going to happen even before I dropped the puck. He would skate toward an opposing defence-man, slide the puck along the ice, and insert it between the skates of the towering defender. The defenceman would look down for a split second to find the puck, and in that little time

Gretzky was around him and in on the net, with the puck cradled on his stick.

The problem I had in other games in which I refereed the Oilers was trying not to become a fan, watching Wayne's exploits instead of watching the game. (I had the same problem a few years earlier with Bobby Orr. I'd watch Orr until someone would foul him and the yells of the Boston faithful would bring me back to my job.) It was really something to be able to follow the play up the ice and watch Gretzky create and set up a play. Then someone would foul him and I'd say, "Hey, that's a penalty!" and then I'd suddenly remember that I was the guy who was supposed to call the penalties. I think all officials in all sports can't help but watch the superstars from time to time. I'm sure NBA referees often took a moment to enjoy watching Michael Jordan glide through the air.

As great as he was, Gretzky wasn't above whining to the referees, although he and every other player would probably call it "enlightening the referee." He was the captain of the Oilers, and complaining to the officials was part of his job. He would often approach me and tell me what he felt wasn't right in a particular game. The problem was that he was right 95 percent of the time, except when he was looking for an edge for his team. But being a typical referee, I wasn't going to let him tell me how to run the game. I did, however, remember what he told me for future games.

Wayne dominated hockey as a player. He did everything so well. He didn't have the presence of a Jean Beliveau, the legendary Montreal Canadien, or Bobby Orr, or Bobby Hull, the type of players who really stood out for how they did one thing very well. Wayne went one step further and made everyone around him a much better player.

In my first book, *Calling the Shots*, which came out when Wayne was playing for Los Angeles, I made some comments about him that I still believe are true:

> He controls the game as much with his mind as with his physical skills. He can read the play far in advance and seems to know what the other players are going to do before they know themselves. Actually, he does control and dominate a game like Beliveau did, but doesn't stand out. Is Gretzky the best player I ever saw? That's hard to say, because he isn't as spectacular as many of his predecessors. As far as having a feel for the game, there has been no one better. There have been better skaters, better shooters, and better stickhandlers but none of them were able to have put it all together like Gretzky has. He does it all, both on and off the ice, and has been a great asset to the game of hockey.

●

Hockey needs more men like Wayne Gretzky. No one could match him in talent, but I see no reason why every player, especially the superstars, can't be his equal in grace and diplomacy. He was and is the epitome of what athletes should strive to be, both on and off the playing surface.

We can learn everything we need to know about Wayne Gretzky from the way he retired. Earlier in the season, he knew he was going to retire, but he didn't want to announce it because it would have become a distraction to his team, the New York Rangers, who were after a playoff spot. Gretzky's intentions leaked out into the press a week before the end of the season, but he didn't officially announce his retirement until just before his final game of the season. He surely didn't want a farewell season, in which the accolades would get out of control. He just wanted one game to say goodbye, and thank you.

As I watched him skate around the ice in his very last game, on April 18, 1999, I was thinking the same way. Thanks, Wayne.

diehards and bandwagon jumpers

17

I 've always been fascinated by fan loyalty. Fans become attached to a team from game one of a franchise, and from that point on, no matter where that person lives, their loyalty never falters.

Fans quickly jumped on the bandwagon in cities such as Edmonton and Winnipeg in the early 1980s. (Of course in Edmonton they had good reason to cheer.) The fans in Edmonton and Winnipeg had mixed emotions every time the Toronto Maple Leafs or Montreal Canadiens came to town. For so many years, they had likely been huge fans of the Leafs or Canadiens because they watched them every Saturday on *Hockey Night in Canada*.

They had grown up on Beliveau and Keon, and now they had great players in their own backyard, Wayne Gretzky and Mark Messier in Edmonton and Dale Hawerchuk in Winnipeg.

At first, there were often more cheers for the Leafs or the Canadiens than the home team when they skated onto the ice. But once the home team got going, the fans soon fell in love with their new team.

It was the same in Vancouver. I remember going to there to referee a Canuck game against Toronto in 1970. I had refereed their games when they were in the Western Hockey League also, and they had a pretty good fan following, but when the Leafs came to town, you'd think you were watching the Stanley Cup playoffs.

It was the same in Calgary, after the Flames moved there from Atlanta. Whenever Toronto or Montreal were in town, interest in the game soared. There were lots of Leaf or Canadiens jerseys in the stands. Oh sure, interest in the game would increase for the other Original Six teams — the Bruins, Red Wings, Rangers, or Blackhawks — but the Leafs and Canadiens were by far the most popular visiting teams.

Many old-timers living in cities like Edmonton and Vancouver still have a strong allegiance to Montreal and Toronto, even though their local teams have far surpassed them at this point — Edmonton winning a few Stanley Cups, and Calgary one also. What have the Leafs done lately, or the Canadiens either for that matter? But these old-time teams are still in the hearts of many diehard fans.

Leaf fans really got their money's worth with the exciting

brand of hockey that coach Pat Quinn had them playing in 1998–99. I tuned in to watch their games and enjoyed myself for the first time in many years. They made good use of the ice. They were a throwback to those Oiler teams of the early 1980s. Maybe the Leafs' style will rub off on more teams for the 1999–2000 season. Wouldn't that be a treat! I'm sorry to say that I can't say the same for the Canadiens, who had a dismal 1998–99. My feeling is that the Original Six teams should always be top contenders in the league and maintain their tradition as leaders. Alas, it is not to be so.

I'm always surprised at the level of the fan dedication and loyalty to a team, even though that team might have had a losing record for a number of years. My son Randy breathes, sleeps, and eats thinking of Maple Leaf blue and white. Leaf paraphernalia is everywhere in his home and at his office. Often, he manages to include a Maple Leaf symbol somewhere on his clothing. We get into the act too. We usually buy him a Leaf-related item for his birthday and Christmas. Randy's sons have continued the family tradition and are collecting their own Leafs stuff.

I think this kind of fan loyalty is great, even if I don't understand it. Maybe my career as a referee has given me a different perspective than the average fan. I just enjoy good hockey, no matter who is playing.

In the playoffs, though, Leaf coach Pat Quinn decided that the Leafs were playing a different season, and that they could no longer play the wide-open style that had given them so much success in the regular season. They tried to frustrate their opponents with a close-checking system and to pop in a goal when the other team let down their guard.

The Leafs made it to the conference finals playing this style of hockey, but lost out to the defensive-minded Buffalo Sabres and their outstanding goalie, Dominik Hasek. Still, Leaf fans, who have had to endure a Cup drought of 32 years and counting, were delighted by the Cup run. Many Leaf fans have ridden a roller coaster with the Leafs since 1967 and were rewarded by the Leaf success in 1999, when many new fans jumped on the Leaf bandwagon. It was a great time for the franchise, and a reward for their well-deserving fans.

●

When I first started to referee pro hockey, I was shocked by the number of busloads of fans who had travelled hundreds of miles to see their team play in other cities. But then I think back to my intermediate-hockey playing days as a kid in Milton, and I remember the excitement of visiting another town, and the fun the fans had in cheering us on in an enemy rink.

One time during the early 1950s, our local team was in the playoffs against a team from Collingwood, Ontario. Milton fans booked an entire train so they could make the trip to Collingwood several hours north to cheer our team on. Television hadn't yet arrived so the local intermediate team was everything to the hockey fans of the era (except for listening to Foster Hewitt's broadcast the Leaf games on radio, perhaps). This was the only way our diehard fans could watch us in action. Otherwise, we would have been sorely outnumbered by the Collingwood fans.

The fans are what the game of hockey is all about, just as in any sport. The game is played for the entertainment of the fans, and for the most part, they appreciate good, clean hockey, and of course they always want their team to win.

Some fans aren't satisfied with great hockey, though. They'd rather watch the goons duke it out. Thankfully, those fans are increasingly becoming the minority. Maybe their interest in good hockey has waned somewhat because of the boring tight-checking style of today. Or maybe they've never had the opportunity to watch a game played at a high level of skill. The NHL hasn't seen a lot of that kind of game in a long time, so the young fans have never had the opportunity to see how the game should really be played. North American hockey programs have been dominated by defensive-minded training for quite some time. I think it's high time we show the next generation of fans why they should really cheer.

part 4
cause for hope

the top 18
(and bottom) 20

I've spent a lot of time in this book pointing out what's wrong with hockey. But don't worry — I haven't forgotten that hockey is the greatest sport in the world. There's no doubt in my mind. Below, I list the Top 20 things about hockey. I also list the Bottom 20, as well. After all, a referee has to be fair!

The Top Twenty

1   Speed. Hockey is the fastest team sport in the world. Don't even try to argue that one with me. The speed of the game makes it the most exciting of the major sports. The other

sports aren't as fast, but they do have their own charm —
baseball is slow, but full of history; basketball comes down
to the last two minutes, and has a lot of time-outs; in football, they spend more time not playing than actually playing;
and soccer, is . . . well, soccer.

2 The pre-game warm-up. The warm-up is such a simple thing
and the fans don't pay much attention, but it's worth watching. For one thing, the players don't usually wear helmets, so
it gives the fans a chance to see exactly what the players look
like. Most teams work out their lines during the warm-up, so
you get a preview of who will be playing together during the
game.

3 Penalty shots. Picture it: Paul Kariya's been hooked on his
way to the net, and the referee gives him a penalty shot. He
circles at his blueline and strides through centre ice cradling
the puck on his stick. He looks down at the goalie, who shuf-
fles back and forth between the pipes. Kariya pushes off and
stickhandles his way over the blueline. The goalie moves out
of the net and taps his stick on the ice and waits for Kariya
. . . What could be better than that?

4 Overtime in the playoffs. It could go on for two hours, or it
could go on for two minutes. But whatever the length of
time, the fans are on the edges of their seats every second of
play.

5 Hockey on the radio. I especially love listening to hockey
broadcasts while driving in my car. If you ever get the chance
to hear Joe Bowen, the radio voice of the Toronto Maple
Leafs, you know what I'm talking about. He can even make

an icing call exciting. I also enjoy Buffalo Sabre play-by-play man Rick Jeanneret. Every time Buffalo scores a goal, you'd think Jeanneret had just won a million bucks. And now, thanks to the Internet, you can listen to hockey on radio from every city in North America!

6 *Hockey Night in Canada.* It's an institution in Canada, and for good reason. Some of the happiest days of my childhood were spent huddled around the television watching the Toronto Maple Leafs, the Montreal Canadiens, the Boston Bruins, the New York Rangers, the Chicago Blackhawks, and the Detroit Red Wings battle it out on Saturday nights. Like many Canadians, I have fond memories of Foster Hewitt shouting, "He shoots! He scores!"

7 Don Cherry, Ron McLean, and "Coach's Corner." Whether you agree with him or not, and usually I don't, there's no doubt he's popular and creates interest in the game. Mind you, his views on the game, especially on fighting and Europeans, are harmful to the game. But his passion for hockey is nearly unparalleled.

8 Video replay. The referees don't much enjoy it when the scoreboard shows that they've made the wrong call, and the fans razz them, but then again the scoreboard shows when they're right, too. For the fans attending the games and paying the big bucks, getting to see the replay of a goal adds to the entertainment value, especially when they have to sit through television time-outs.

9 Intermission features. See my discussion of "Coach's Corner." Every city has its own brand of intermission

entertainment, whether it be interviews, short features on players, or discussions with media pundits. In Chicago, they always pick a great-looking woman out of the crowd to shoot pucks for prizes.

10 Referees. Just kidding!

11 The Quebec International Peewee Tournament. Teams from all over the world come to compete in the most prestigious of all kids' tournaments. The kids get to meet other kids from all over and can watch different ways of playing the game.

12 Pick-up hockey. When kids or adults simply show up to play a game, they're there just to have fun. Rarely do they take the game too seriously and engage in nonsense, as they do when they're playing for real.

13 Wayne Gretzky. The man is what hockey is all about — grace, passion, courtesy, intensity.

14 The All-Star Game. Usually the game isn't anything like a regular game — there's no hitting, and lots of scoring. But the celebrations and the tributes to the legends of the game are truly enjoyable. The playmaking is exceptional — the talented players are allowed to show their true puck-handling and passing skills without being hauled down.

15 The amateur draft. Even though most of the players who are drafted will never make it to the NHL, and the top players are a couple of years away, it's exciting for the fans to watch teams select their future stars and make last-minute deals to move up the board and pick the next great player.

16 International hockey. The Olympics, the World Cup of Hockey, the World Junior championships — now that's great hockey. Men and women compete against the elite from other countries and put on a fantastic show.

17 The Stanley Cup. There is no more recognizable trophy in professional team sports. No Cup celebration is complete until the members of the winning teams skate around the ice and pass the trophy to each other and take turns hoisting it high over their heads.

18 Hockey Hall of Fame. I'm talking about the actual site, as opposed to the institution, which has a long way to go to make up for poor past decisions, not the least of which was voting me down when I was nominated! (That may not have been their worst decision ever, but there were definitely some people on the committee who did not want me in there.) But the Hall is a wonderful celebration of hockey and appeals to fans of all ages. They have some fantastic exhibits and memorabilia.

19 Mario Lemieux, Jean Beliveau, Jaromir Jagr, Wayne Gretzky, and Bobby Orr. Each of them deserves his own entry on this list. These men are hockey's true greats.

20 The popularity of minor-pro hockey in the United States. These teams go all out. The fans are really into these games. The success of teams in American cities shows us just how much the image of the game is changing south of the border.

Honourable mention: The Hockey News. No other publication in any sport covers its game in such a comprehensive and responsible way.

Honourable mention II: Hockey pools. What a great way

for the fans to get into the game and to get into heated discussions.

The Bottom Twenty

1 Too much noise. When I was refereeing they didn't need to have loud rock music blasting away at the end of each whistle. Mind you, if they had, I wouldn't have heard the fans calling me every name you can imagine, so maybe it's a good thing, too.

2 Don Cherry and "Coach's Corner." He's also on the Top 20 list. If you ever saw me skate over and have a chat with Cherry at the Boston bench, you'll understand why he's on this list, too.

3 The hockey season finishing in late June. Yes, you can get too much of a good thing. When interest in the game should be at its peak, viewership is on the decline. The season is just too long.

4 Too much time between playoff series. Schedules should be set up so that when one round ends early, they can adjust the schedule and get right to the next one. They could have cut a week off the season if they had done that in 1998–99.

5 Too many advertising time-outs. They're okay if you're watching the game on television, but if you're at the game, any excitement that has built up is brought to a screaming halt.

6 The high cost of playing minor hockey. It's difficult for kids from middle- or lower-income homes to afford to play at the highest levels. Unfortunately, some kids have no choice but to stop playing organized hockey.

7 Fighting. You already know what I think about fighting — it's not a necessary part of the game.

8 Canadian teams folding due to financial difficulty. Small-market Canadian teams simply can't compete against the wealthy teams around the league. We've already lost the Quebec Nordiques and the Winnipeg Jets. Watching those Winnipeg fans wave goodbye to their team was hard.

9 Expansion. I used to know who every player was in the league. Now, it's nearly impossible. There are too many teams, too many players, and too few stars on each team. When there are already so many teams in financial difficulty, why add more? It's a cash cow for the NHL.

10 The high cost of going to games. Ticket prices are skyrocketing (even if a team isn't doing well), parking's a fortune, and of course you can't go to a game without buying souvenirs and food. It's getting to be that only the affluent can afford to go to games.

11 The neutral zone trap, and other defence-oriented systems. They're the bane of hockey. They eliminate scoring and shut down the freewheeling players.

12 Hero worship of goons. These players can do little else than throw fists.

13 The game is too organized. There are too many systems — offence, defence, penalty killing, line match-ups. The spontaneity of creative, exciting plays is lost in all the structure.

14 Negative parents. In minor hockey, some parents become too involved and fail to be supportive of their kids, the coaches, and the officials. These parents need to lay off and let the

kids do their stuff. They should support their kids and shout words of encouragement, not of criticism.

15 High salaries. Do the guaranteed millions the players earn affect their performance? Does playing for personal gain affect their hunger for winning for the team? I'm afraid it might.

16 The image of hockey as a violent sport. The goon era still lingers. Some people still think of hockey as roller derby on ice. We need to clean up the violence if we hope to attract a larger fan base.

17 Player holdouts. In recent years, some of the biggest names in the game have refused to play, sometimes in the middle of their contract, over salary disputes. This alienates the fans and puts the focus on money rather than the game.

18 The trading deadline. The deadline is far too late in the season and allows for rent-a-player scenarios — teams can acquire soon-to-be free agents from non-playoff bound teams in their quest to win the Stanley Cup. Teams should shore up their teams at least a month before the end of the season so that they can't pick up hired guns late.

19 The abuse of young players. This problem has been in the news a lot, with the trials of former coach Graham James and some staff at Maple Leaf Gardens, and Sheldon Kennedy talking openly about the abuse he suffered. Kids are now much more aware of the problem, however.

20 TV highlight reels glorifying fighting. We got away from that for a while, but they seem to be coming back.

at the summits and beyond 19

The 1991 Summit

The late Danny Gallivan, the legendary voice of the Montreal Canadiens on *Hockey Night in Canada* who coined such fabulous phrases as "cannonading drive" and "Savardian spinorama," made one statement at the 1991 Hockey Summit held in Toronto that said it all: "NHL hockey — elevates mediocrity, punishes excellence."

Gallivan's comment wasn't on topic for that particular summit, but we all heard what he had said and saw merit in it. It was a very honest and true evaluation. What he said is thought by many, but voiced by few.

The 1991 Hockey Summit, subtitled "For the Love of the Game," was put together by the Fair Play in Sport Commission for Canada, of which I was a member. The lead items on the agenda at the summit were violence in hockey, the lack of respect for the game and the officials in it, and the overall image of hockey.

The Fair Play in Sport Commission had been formed five years earlier in 1986 by the Canadian federal government when people began to realize that there's too much violence in sports, not just ice hockey. I volunteered to participate on the commission as soon as I heard about it. I saw being on the commission as a chance to contribute to the movement to put fun back into the game of hockey.

The intent of the commission was to put into place a "values framework for sport," to demonstrate "attitudes and behaviour in sport consistent with the belief that sport is an ethical and humane pursuit." Pretty heavy stuff, I know. I'll translate for you: "to make athletes, all members of the sport community, parents, and teachers aware that integrity, sportsmanship, and honesty remain the most important ingredients of any sport." Think of that statement, and compare it to our methods of teaching hockey to our young people these days. You can see that we had our work cut out for us, even with the Great One, Wayne Gretzky, as our first honorary chairman.

●

I gave a report to the commission at the time based on a number of sources. I had talked with parents, coaches, players, referees, and sports people in general, including some at the pro level. Here are my findings:

1. The rules of hockey, although generally having a standard interpretation across the country, are not applied in a standard manner. Many varying levels of application in all areas of the game and of the country cause much frustration to players, coaches, officials, and fans.

2. Players generally do not accept that body-checking is part of the game. Players have a get-even attitude when checked, an attitude that is condoned by his coach, his manager, his peers, and likely his parents.

3. Parents in particular, coaches, and managers, fail to accept the rulings of the officials, and set a poor example by berating and chastising the official for the call, therefore setting the example for the young players that this is the way it is supposed to be. They then maintain that realm of thinking as they grow into becoming become parents, coaches, and managers themselves.

4. There is a lack of firm standard in the areas of hooking, holding, interference — the restraining fouls — and this causes the players much frustration, to the point of discouraging them from playing their best, or to reacting in a violent way — to cross-check, slash, charge, or even engage in fisticuffs. It is this type of play that causes the long games with continual pushing and shoving after the whistle stop establishes supremacy.

5. The big brother syndrome, more often referred to as the "goon squad," is far too prevalent in the game — the attitude

of "don't you check me or you-know-who will come onto the ice and get even on the next shift" has changed the structure of hockey. Again. The lack of rule application, the failure to accept that body-checking is a part of the game, has led the sport into falsely believing that every team has to carry an equalizer.

Sound familiar? Most of this is still going on, and is still a problem. And within the last 10 years we've fostered a devotion to shutting down offensive skills as the number one coaching edict. We're at a crossroad in hockey. We need to alter our course to make a better future for the game, especially for the young players of the future. We were directing our message then at the young people of Canada, the beginners, with hopes of reaching the parents and the coaches as a secondary result. I really wonder how much has been accomplished since we made our findings. We weren't attempting to change the purpose of the game of hockey. We were just trying to get back to the principles of fair play. We weren't trying to take away the opportunity for skills development, or body contact, or the excitement of scoring goals. We were looking to level the playing field for all. Our motto, "Let's Get Back into the Game," could very well be a motto for today.

When I look back to my notes from the 1991 summit, I notice that we talked little about the quality of play of our game. Our intent was to point out how the amount of violence in hockey, especially at the NHL level, affected the overall tempo of the game. We didn't look at coaching methods, the style of play, or the hurtful defensive tactics that had crept into the game at that point. We talked about how well we did in such events as the Canada Cup series, the Junior World Championships, and other events. But we didn't talk about how hockey registration among kids was its lowest level in a long time. We simply said that enrollment was down because of a lack of available ice time, the violence in the sport scared some kids away, and there were too many games and practices, causing kids as young as 14 to get out of hockey. But we didn't discuss how hockey isn't fun for kids any more. We now place the emphasis on winning above all else, not on kids enjoying themselves.

Murray Costello, president of the Canadian Amateur Hockey Association (CAHA), was among the participants in this well-publicized event. Murray said that kids were allowed to play too rough in minor hockey. The good players suffered because their talents were inhibited by the rough play. The less talented, hard-hitting kids dominated these potential stars. I agreed with Costello's assessment at the time, and still do.

The emphasis in minor hockey is on playing the body all of the time, not the puck. In other words, we emphasize defensive skills to the detriment of kids' offensive skills. What happens is that youngsters learn how to take out their man, but if they happen to get the puck in the process, they have no clue what to do with it. This mentality is a detriment to our game. The game is supposed to be about getting the puck, stickhandling, passing, taking a shot, not hammering away at the other kids and intimidating them into submission.

Costello also pointed out that Team Canada, featuring many of Canada's elite professional players, knew that in international hockey, fighting was punished by expulsion from the game, so the players abided by that rule. He means, of course, that we could apply that kind of punishment to deter fighting at all levels of hockey, and our players would pay attention and cut down on fighting.

Bob Nicholson, vice-president of technical for the CAHA at the time and currently president of that organization (which is now called the Canadian Hockey Association), also attended the summit. Nicholson is an advocate of better coaching and training for kids at a younger age. He's suggested splitting the ice surface into two or three rinks for the younger set. They took his suggestion, and still use it today.

Gary Green, a former coach in major junior hockey and the NHL, and currently a television hockey analyst, talked about the importance of a young hockey player's first coach. Green believes that the coach is the first person to tell a player how the game should be played. The role of that person is so important because bad habits can develop right from the start. If a coach teaches only defence, players won't be given the opportunity to develop their natural offensive talents because they're too busy trying to shut down other good players. Many coaches preach the value of corralling good players, of not allowing them to get free and make plays. These coaches teach tactics that are on the verge of being against the rules. Only the best players can break the harness of all-out defensive training and become effective professional players.

Green believes that fighting is not necessarily a part of hockey. He believes so strongly that fighting should be eliminated in the sport that he was willing to fight for it — he nearly came to blows with Don Cherry in the lobby of a Canadian hotel when the two discussed the matter. (A couple of the officials in town for the game witnessed it and thought they might have to go into action early.) While Green acknowledged that fighting will likely always be in professional hockey, he feels that glorifying fighting the way Cherry does is not good for the game, and that people should actively discourage fisticuffs instead. (In a survey I carried out through a local weekly newspaper in 1991, answered by a number of parents and hockey fans, the general consensus was that fighting had no place in the game of hockey. Some disagreed, and said fighting was a safe release of frustration in the game, but they were outnumbered four to one. Only one respondent claimed that fighting is a part of hockey.)

The International Ice Hockey Federation was represented at the summit by its vice-president, Gordon Renwick. He informed us that international hockey was enjoying great success, with improved communication between coaches and the officials, and a better training program for the referees that gives them back some of the control of the game. It was a nice statement, but really it was a case of wishful thinking. They had and still have a ways to go to catch up to the quality of North American officiating. On one hand, I hope they catch up to us, but on the other, I hope they don't learn, as our officials have, to let so much of the clutching and grabbing go.

What I found most interesting about the summit was a report from Brian O'Neill, who represented the NHL. O'Neill stated that if you eliminate fighting from hockey, the amount of stick-work will increase to the point that the referees won't bother to call infractions for slashing and hooking and the like. O'Neill's comment makes me think that the referees certainly aren't in charge of the game on the ice. In fact, I'm sure of it. Otherwise, I wouldn't have suffered the abuse I did as a referee and since for suggesting that we improve hockey, and increase the role of the referee to gain back control of the game. When I was a referee, we were expected to stay in line and to do as we were told. Our instructions didn't come from higher-level officials, who should have been instructing us, but from league brass.

O'Neill also commented that fans love to watch fights. Why else would television make NHL fights such a big part in of their highlight packages? O'Neill believes that fans dislike stick fouls (which would increase, he believes, if fighting is abolished) and don't mind players taking penalties as much for fighting as they do for stick infractions. O'Neill's one saving grace was that he agreed that fighting as a tactic to goad and intimidate should be abolished.

In his report on the summit, O'Neill noted that, "the NHL is a business, and our business is entertainment of which the product is hockey, the most exciting sport in the world." He stressed what he believed to be the three main factors of NHL hockey, and I quote:

- The intensity and emotion of the game being played at the pinnacle of athletic skill in a confined circumstance of time and space
- The highest expression of the artistic form of the sport
- The competitive factor

O'Neill said that the grinding, defensive system in which the NHL plays allows for the underdog to achieve, therefore making it exciting for everybody because even the lesser-talented teams have a chance against the top dogs.

The spirit of the second and third items on O'Neill's list appears to have been lost along the way. Really, the game now is about the first point, about hockey being played at its pinnacle in a confined space. I'm reminded again about what Gallivan said: "The NHL elevates mediocrity, punishes excellence."

Bob Goodenow, the director of the NHLPA, stated in his address to the summit that his association's purposes included "promoting and fostering the best interests of hockey . . . [the] continued support and advancement of hockey in existing, and into new hockey communities." Goodenow, in the spirit of the summit, brought out the popular phrase, "Last night I went to a boxing match and a hockey game broke out." He said that we have to fix that image of hockey. He also stressed the need to curb the amount of stick work and the further violence that stick infractions spawn.

No one at the summit discussed what Goodenow hinted at, about what leads to violent acts: illegal use of a stick, interference, and clutching and grabbing. Because players aren't able to demonstrate their offensive skills, they become frustrated, and fight back the only way they know how — with their sticks. We discussed the violence, but we didn't discuss how it all begins. It wasn't even addressed as an "item of importance" on the summit's agenda. Apparently, no one saw a reason to explore this issue.

Only in the last few years, with the influx of European players, the reduction in scoring, the abundance of boring hockey games, and our poor showing in international competition have we come to realize the need to reassess the game and the way it is played.

The 1999 Summit

Change, change, change!

This is what two-thirds of Canadians want to see in hockey, according to a poll taken across Canada in conjunction with the Open Ice Hockey Summit held in Toronto in the summer of 1999. The three-day conference had representatives from the National Hockey League, Canadian Hockey Association, and Canadian Hockey League. Leaf general manager Ken Dryden, Wayne Gretzky, Bob Gainey, general manager of the Dallas Stars, and Colin Campbell, vice-president of the NHL, were in attendance. As well, more than 100 hockey parents and minor hockey coaches were invited to participate. I don't know whether any referees participated in the summit, or if anyone spoke on behalf of referees. In fact, I saw the word "refereeing" exactly twice in reams of reports I read about the summit. I'm sure that everyone in attendance felt they had all the answers, so what more could a referee add?

Unlike the 1991 summit, I observed this gathering from a distance. I followed it closely in the major newspapers, and listened to extensive radio and television coverage. I read and saw what concerned hockey fans read and saw. My concern for the future of hockey began long before this summit was organized, and I was interested in seeing what recommendations these people would come up with.

What I found most interesting about the conference was that there was no discussion of violence, fighting, or intimidation — what I feel to be the most important issues in the game today. There was lots of talk about putting fun back into hockey. Wayne Gretzky, the honorary chair of the summit, mentioned it at the beginning. I agreed with The Great One when he said that we need to get away from teaching defensive systems, and that we need to stress creativity. He also wisely stated that kids need more practice time instead of simply playing games, at least a one to one ratio. What a breath of fresh air! But were people listening to what he had to say? It's all window dressing if the suggestions that were put forth go unheeded.

For the most part, the observations at the summit were obvious ones. For instance, the talent level of our Canadian youngsters has dropped below that of their European counterparts. The participants found that European children "learn and practice their skills more," having fewer games and more actual practice time.

I find it interesting that the International Ice Hockey Federation distributes Canadian coaching manuals and related materials to its member countries. Does this mean we know what needs to be done? Probably not. With our win-win attitude, we forget the most important lessons we can teach our young hockey players — skills, teamwork, discipline, concentration, intensity, and camaraderie. Not only are these important hockey skills, but they're essential in developing youngsters' character. We are so driven to win — we fear losing. Our kids learn to shut down the "A" players with "C"-level tactics — closing down the lanes and checking, checking, checking.

Back to the rough stuff — the violence, fighting, and intimidation. Hockey is often played now on the edge of mayhem, and not just in the NHL. At any age, the level of intimidation by many players, coaches, and even parents is enough to shut down the kids' creativity and imagination in the game. There was no mention of violence and intimidation at the summit. If there was, it sure didn't make it into the press, and we all know the media covers everything.

Unfortunately, the three-day 1999 summit was a superficial overview of the game of hockey. Everyone was too macho, subscribing to the idea that you mustn't speak up about fighting or the rough side of the game, or everyone will think you're a softie. You can't look like a loser for the hockey crowd, you know.

During the summit there wasn't much time devoted to why we play the game, our attitudes about the game, and what they hoped to accomplish at the summit. If they had, I am sure that violence, fighting, and intimidation tactics would have been front and centre.

Another area discussed at the summit is the need to address practices — to involve lots of skills training, but in a fun way. It's important that kids get the opportunity to apply their skills in scrimmages during practice time. In scrimmages, youngsters get the chance to do some things with the puck that they would likely never get to attempt in a game situation. After all, it might be too costly. The opposing team might take advantage of an error by that player in attempting to perfect a new skill and score a goal. Heaven forbid! If kids aren't given the opportunity to learn in a game situation, how will they ever gain confidence in their ability to manoeuvre about the ice with the puck creating imaginative plays? Kids need to make mistakes and learn from them under pressure in game situations. The summit really didn't discuss this issue.

One good idea that came out of the event was to establish master coaches, who would be responsible for overseeing a certain number of coaches in an area. I don't think that'll happen. I don't think there will be enough coaches at a high level to whom the other coaches would pay attention. Who would set the standards for these "super coaches?" This would be a big, big task with a lot of merit, but would require rigid standards to teach proper skills and emphasize having fun.

I think that, in addition to a master coach, they should attempt to establish a master referee coach for a given area, someone who could instill a firm standard of no-nonsense refereeing in hockey. League management dictates the standards that prevail in calling a game, but they never seem to agree. Generally, teams will waver on the standard they set at the beginning of a season as the season progresses, based on how their team is doing, not whether a ruling is in the best interest of the game — that comes second. A strong head referee is needed at all levels to stick to the rules. The master referee would support the officials, and not allow them to avoid making calls and let too much crap go on in a game because of pressure brought about by those with the loudest voices. Referees are influenced by these people too often at most levels, and this only damages league credibility.

Another idea put forward at the summit was to tie the schools into hockey programs. I think this would be a wonderful thing for hockey. Not only is ice time more available during the day, but kids can develop school pride as they develop their talents. Why not add hockey to the curriculum? Give students a credit for participating when they reach a certain level. It makes a lot of sense to me. This would encourage girls to play hockey as well. It would be an equal opportunity school program. This is a far cry from when I went to school and it was unheard of for girls to play hockey.

Tying hockey into school programs will help reduce the costs of playing hockey. The high cost is one of the main reasons youngsters are restricted from playing more and developing further.

So how useful was the 1999 summit? Overall, not very useful, other than it got people talking and trying to figure out solutions. That's probably the only thing of value that came out of it. It didn't focus on many areas, but then maybe it wasn't trying to. A good recommendation would have been to hold summits on specific areas of interest more often.

Here's a summary of the recommendations made at the Open Ice Hockey Summit:

- Establish a coaching mentor system. This is a good idea, but one that would likely not work. Coaches tend to think that they know how to coach better than anybody else. If somebody else tells them what to do, they likely won't listen, unless the mentor is a highly respected individual. And there wouldn't be enough mentors for 20 teams. A better idea would be to have a central office that coaches can call if they need help. Coaches are far more likely to take advice when it's not forced on them. Coaches could call and ask what they can do about a player with a specific attitude problem. Or they could ask technical questions. The technical advisor could suggest ways for the team to improve, and might even hire roving instructors to come out to practices to help out.
- Increase the practice-to-game ratio. If a player practices more, there's no question his or her skills would improve. The problem is kids don't much enjoy practices, and you're going to lose them. They want to play games. If practices were set up so that they were fun (again, have

scrimmages) the kids would be more likely to keep at it.

● Combine hockey and school. As I already mentioned, it's a great idea to mix sports and education, but there are some pitfalls. The risk is that the extra playing and practice time during school might benefit only the elite players. And other than to reduce the costs of ice-time and to give kids who wouldn't normally have the chance to play the opportunity to get involved, hockey during school might not be needed. After all, the Canadian and American minor hockey systems are rigidly structured. But then again, many places don't have structured junior hockey and would benefit from the extra playing time.

● Raising the draft eligibility age. This is a silly suggestion (at least for the NHL). Eventually the rule would be chal-lenged in court and the NHL would lose, as has happened in the past. If players are in over their heads, playing at too high a level, it's hard to say whether or not that hurts them. As it stands now, an individual certainly has a choice. The athletes and their parents should determine if a player is ready to move on to the next level.

Will hockey benefit from hearing from hockey's heavies at the 1999 summit? It's hard to say now. But at least the door to thinking about the future of hockey has been opened. If enough influential people get a more realistic view of what the game is all about, maybe we can get our game back on track.

The 1991 and 1999 summits haven't been the only forums for fixing hockey. Earlier in 1999, the creation of a new youth hockey program was announced. Hall of Famers Bobby Orr and Mike Bossy, and Cassie Campbell of the Canadian Women's National Team, will stress responsibility and respect for others. The program will hold Safe and Fun Hockey Camps to help get out their message. Orr noted in the press conference held to announce the plans that we need to look at the state of the game. He mentioned recent events in which police had to be called in to resolve on-ice violence and confrontations that take place outside the rinks.

Mike Bossy said, "A lot of the problem in the game today is the attitude is wrong." He indicated that through the new program, they hope to change that attitude, and give kids life-long values that will help them in sport and in other aspects of their lives.

In 1997, the Citizenship Through Sports Alliance was created. Nine major U.S. sport organizations, including all four major pro team sports, the NCAA, and the U.S. Olympic Committee got together to set a mandate to promote the positive values in sport. "Sports in America is really a reflection of our society," stated Cedric Dempsey, the executive director of the NCAA. Very true. Sport does mirror society. The trick is to break that tie. NBA commissioner David Stern said that the group wasn't formed to deal with "individual transgressions," but to foster respect, fair play, and ethical behaviour among the thousands of kids and millions of fans reached by any particular sport.

NHL commissioner Gary Bettman noted the Alliance was just one of the ways of getting out a more focused message. A number of organizations need to spread the word. "We are engaged . . . in collective consciousness raising," stated Bettman. He mentioned that he was working with organizations in Canada to promote the same message.

A report by the Canadian Hockey League compared the state of hockey in 1991 to that of 10 years earlier. They found that the quality of the game had increased. Improvements and development in the areas of coaching, training, and conditioning mean that today's athletes are more highly skilled, and are better equipped to meet the challenges of the game. But the report also noted, "One of the negative developments in the game has been the sophisticated methods that are now employed to impede the more skilled players by reason of the various 'pick plays' and various blocking methods."

Right on, CHL! They picked up on that 10 years ago, and now it's happening more than ever. Let's hope they add it to the agenda of the next summit.

the game never stops changing 20

You can't convince Buffalo fans it should have counted, and Dallas fans aren't interested because they have the Stanley Cup.

I got many phone calls from radio and television people asking for my comments on Brett Hull's Cup-winning goal the day after the playoffs ended. Three radio stations called me in one day! It's funny, even people who didn't know I had been an NHL referee asked me, "Was it a good goal or not?"

To recap, Brett Hull was in the crease when he scored the 1999 Stanley Cup–winning goal in overtime. Video replays showed that. But the NHL ruled that Hull had possession of the puck, which meant that the goal was allowed to stand.

Any goal as controversial as that one should have been taken under review. But the thing was, after Dallas scored, the press flooded out onto the ice, and the Stars went crazy celebrating their win. With all the mayhem going on, the league didn't review the goal. Their credibility took a big hit. Clearly, the NHL feared the repercussions of calling the goal back, so their decision came under suspicion.

The league did go on a media blitz over the next couple of days explaining that it was in fact a goal and that it had been reviewed. They also noted that this very situation had been clarified to the teams just weeks before.

My reply when asked about the goal is to turn it around and ask what the person who asked the question thought about the goal. Almost everyone says it was no goal. The consensus is that had the goal been scored in the first period, it would likely have been disallowed.

I'm not so sure of that. That would have been a different situation, though, and might have been interpreted differently than it would have in overtime. The way it happened, there was no decision made upstairs. Once the puck was in the net, the game was over. The usual protocol is to go upstairs to allow or disallow a goal, but this didn't take place. That's why there's so much second-guessing going on.

Hockey fans are generally just disgusted by the mess. They wish the toe-in-crease rule had never been introduced. Leave it up to the refs, they say. At least we can blame them, like back in the good old days.

Throughout the course of the season, I must have been asked a million times about the controversial crease replay rule. People ask what I would call if a player's toe is in the crease. Under the rules of the day, I wouldn't have to call a goal or no-goal. I could just defer upstairs for the final decision.

In a Pittsburgh-Toronto game in the 1999 playoffs, referee Kerry Fraser had to make a ruling on a goal in just such a situation. A Pittsburgh shot on the Toronto net got in behind goalie Curtis Joseph, hit one goal post, proceeded along the goal line, hit either the inside of the post (which would make it a goal) or the post (no goal), and squirted back into play.

Play was whistled down. Fraser did not indicate if a goal had been scored. Instead, he went upstairs for the answer, as so commonly happened throughout the season. The video officials could even call down to the referee before play had resumed to say, "Hold things up while we review that last play." Then they'd tell the referee what the result was and he'd have to act accordingly.

Not in this situation, however. The video judge couldn't make a decision. Nor could the series supervisor or the director of officiating. It was left up to Fraser to decide. He called it a goal. He made his decision based on what he believed he saw and from talking to the goal judge. It was not a popular decision for the Leafs or their fans. The Leafs went on to win the series, but Fraser's call was a topic of conversation for days and weeks and still comes up when "that rule" is discussed.

Well, "that rule" no longer exists. Just days after that final Stanley Cup game, the league brass kicked the toe-in-the-crease rule out of the books. Video will no longer determine if a player was in the crease. It will be left up to the referees to make the decision, and rightly so. A toe in the crease should not be a reason to call off a goal.

Contact with a goalie should not be the sole reason to disallow a goal, but any type of interference that may cause a distraction for the goalkeeper should be called. Further, any activity of his own accord by the opposing player in the crease should be penalized right away, or we risk open season on the goalies again. The rules are there to guard against that, and they need to be applied.

I remember the exchanges between John Ferguson, when he was a member of the Montreal Canadiens, and goalie Gerry Cheevers of the Boston Bruins. As the play moved out of the Boston zone, Ferguson would make an arc from his wing position and cut through the crease. He wouldn't necessarily make contact with Cheevers, but he would stir up Cheevers, who would sometimes chase Ferguson all the way to the blueline. Harassing the goalie is nothing new, but with today's bigger and faster players, a goalie could be knocked flying during such a rush.

The NHL should alter the rules so that an attacking player can't position himself in front of the net. Perhaps the league should adopt a rule similar to the NBA's three-in-the-key rule, by which a player can't stay in the zone for longer than three seconds before play is called. That would open up play in front of the goalie and would keep skaters out of his face. It would also allow players to skate more in the offensive zone and to set up better shots instead of just peppering the net. The action would no longer be bunched up in the corners, and there wouldn't be any more scrums in front of the net with players piling on top of the goalie.

In the early 1980s, in a game I refereed at Maple Leaf Gardens in Toronto, I called off a Leaf goal because a Leaf player was in the Chicago crease. The non-call cost the Leafs at least a tie with the Blackhawks. In those days the Leafs were not a very good team and had to scratch and tug and pull for just about every win they got, and there weren't a lot of them.

I was once more an unpopular guy in Toronto. I always seemed to get stuck with refereeing bad games in Toronto that made me look bad. The hockey was so bad, I couldn't do anything to make it better. What can you do when home players take dumb penalties and the fans get angry? Yes, there were nights when a game stunk so bad that I couldn't possibly call a good game, especially with players taking penalties every other whistle. Instead of hustling to get the puck, they'd hook each other from behind or grab each other's stick (now written in the book as a penalty), or trip somebody needlessly, or deliberately stop play by freezing the puck against the boards.

Then there were those nights when I could look bad all on my own, too. Not because of what the players were doing, but by my own misjudgment — lack of concentration, or not being into the game, not having a feel for it. I didn't have too many of those nights, thank goodness, or I wouldn't have lasted 21 years as an employee of the NHL.

Anyway, on that particular night at the Gardens, the Chicago Blackhawks were up 3–2 on the Leafs. Late in the game, there was a face-off on the spot to the right of Murray Bannerman, the Chicago goaltender. As soon as the puck was dropped, Leaf forward Jim Korn went right to the Hawk net to prepare to block the goalie's view, or perhaps deflect the puck into the net on a shot. However, the player was overenthusiastic and took it too far. Remember, this was before the use of video replay for toe-in-crease violations, when lots of goals were scored with opposing players in the crease. The Leaf player planted himself in behind Hawk defenceman Keith Brown, right in the crease. Now, ordinarily it wouldn't matter that he was in the crease because the "no harm no foul" rule would apply. The team that was scored on would whine, of course — that went with the territory — but the goal would generally stand.

On this occasion, however, when the puck was shot toward the net by Dan Daoust, the skate of the Leaf in the crease made contact with Bannerman's skate as the goalie attempted to move across the net to block the puck. But Bannerman was prevented from doing so in that split second, and the puck went into the net to cheers from the Leaf fans, who didn't get a lot of opportunity to feel victory, much less a tie.

But lo and behold there was this guy out there in the striped shirt, waving off the goal, and to make matters worse, also putting a Leaf player into the penalty box for interference. Well, I can tell you, I was not too popular. I think there are some Maple Leaf fans who still hate me for not liking their team and for having it in for them. I still hear from the odd, stressing the odd, fan periodically. My reply is that it was easy to not like them — they had lousy teams then.

Even my bosses at the time, who would have liked to see the Leaf teams do better because they got a lot of flack for them losing, said, "You probably could have let that one go."

One of the linesmen in the game said at the time, "The right call against the wrong team in the wrong city."

I can tell you I would have loved to have had the opportunity to use video replay on that night. To have been able to go upstairs and get a replay and get the "no goal" call from them, I'd have been off the hook. The media and the fans would have left me alone.

And now with replay gone and the referee again making judgment calls, I wonder how many of these kinds of situations will once again rear their ugly head. I think it would still make sense for the referee to be able to see the video replay when he feels it's necessary to verify his call. He could just step off the ice into a cubicle or into his own dressing room where the video could be set up to view a goal in question. After all, the ref probably witnessed 95 percent of what just took place, so watching the replay would just help him see what he might have missed.

Other games I refereed come to mind in which I would love to have had the video. It's hard for a referee to wave off a goal and get that gnawing feeling inside of him wondering if he's made the right call. You ask yourself, *Did I make a mistake? Did I miss something?* In that split second, you have to make a decision and can only go on what you saw, with your gut instinct.

For me, sometimes the next day my split-second judgment call was proven wrong. I took what I could from the experience, but all you can really do is just move on. You can't dwell on those kinds of misses. You just have to be confident that you did your very best at the time with the info at hand.

When a rule change is put into place it's interesting to watch the reaction of the players and coaches. Usually, they just make the most of the situation, but they also grumble a lot. Those the change affects but who aren't involved in the on-ice action, like the general managers, don't think about if the rule is good for the game, but if it's good for their team. Sometimes it seems they live in the past, and have no interest in the future. That's why general managers have so many problems agreeing on changes — they don't get the whole picture.

There were many mixed emotions about the cancellation of video replay. I wonder if anyone ever asked the officials what they thought, or whether they were asked to help make the decision.

Let the referee make the decision and get on with the game, right or wrong. I guarantee they will be right many, many more times than they'll be wrong. At least the fans will know right away what the call is and can cheer or boo without having to wait.

Well, folks, an awful lot has changed in the game. The naysayers out there talk about not wanting to change the fabric of the game, just as they have for the past 30 years. Just about every rule has been altered, added to, or interpreted and applied differently. A lot more crap goes on in the game now than ever. Hockey is different from what it was when I got into the game.

But why not change it? Why not try something different to add some excitement in a different way?

For instance, there's nothing wrong with each team earning a point in a tie, as will happen in the 1999–2000 season. Each team will have worked hard to earn that point, so why not give them their reward, and let them fight four on four for the extra point? Four on four hockey is so exciting! I think that's a great change. A goal was scored in only one of four overtime NHL games in 1998–99, so why not give each team its due and give us some flat-out great back-and-forth hockey for five minutes?

The fans will always talk about these rule changes, and ask what ifs. And the coaches like Roger Neilson will look for loopholes in any rule changes, which will lead to further rule changes. The game never stops changing.

For instance, I think the league should go to a shootout if no one scores in overtime. That way, there won't be any ties, and there will always be a winner. And think about how exciting it would be for the fans!

And why not go to larger nets? Why not enlarge the nets, make them bigger than 4 by 6, as they are now? The average size of NHL players has increased, so there are bigger players fighting for more space in front of the net. That means fewer clear shots on net and fewer goals. Increasing the size of the net would mean players could get off clean shots, and scoring would increase, which would increase interest in the game. Add six inches to the height of the net, and six inches to its width. Let's get some scoring back into the game. Let's have more 6–5 games.

A bigger net would encourage the goalkeeper to stay in his crease more, and not to wander out to play the puck. It would be safer for the goalies. After all, how can a goalie get checked if he's not out of the net? They could use rules similar to NFL rules that protect the quarterback. The quarterback is usually safe when he stays in the pocket, and the goalie would be safe as long as he stayed in his crease. While he's playing the puck outside his crease, players should be allowed to check the goalie as they would any other skater. But the minute the goalie shoots the puck away, he should become untouchable, unless he provides a block for his teammate, for which he would be subject to an interference penalty.

I still think there should be something done to eliminate the use of the trap and any and all such contrivances to shut down scoring. The NHL game is becoming like half-rink hockey — a team tries to come out of its own zone, and boom, they hit a wall, and they're back in their own zone. Is that exciting hockey?

There are other rules the NHL should consider. Perhaps they should remove the centre red line. That would cut out the two-line offsides and open up the game. Defencemen would have to stay back more in their own zone, rather than up inside the red line to cut off the lanes.

Why not move the bluelines two feet toward centre so there would be more area in the attacking zone to move the puck around? It would mean less jamming the puck along the boards and in the corners. With no centre line, icing the puck would apply only when you shoot the puck from behind your own blueline. This, too, would help to open up the ice more, as the attacking winger racing to the puck would be able to enter the zone faster than the defenceman would be able to get to the loose puck and set up a play. Also, if they instituted automatic icing instead of the race to the puck, a team would have to think more about just dumping in the puck, and they'd set up more intelligent and entertaining plays.

We need to make more use of the entire ice surface, to eliminate roadblocks. We need to create more space to allow playmaking and creativity. If we do that, we'll have good, free-wheeling, exciting hockey.

the european 21
invasion

Remember when former Toronto Maple Leafs' owner
Harold Ballard said that Swede Inge Hammerstrom
could go into a corner with a dozen eggs in his
pocket and not break any of them?

What he said was true, but it was the start of a stereotype of
Europeans that still holds to a large extent today. There have
been Canadian and American players who could skate into a
corner and leave the eggs unbroken, but only the image of the
typical European as soft offensive players has stuck in our
minds. Remember when we called Europeans Chicken Swedes,
or, as Don Cherry refers to them, Swede Hearts?

Borje Salming and Inge Hammerstrom were the first two prominent European imports to the NHL, in the 1973–74 season. The WHA followed quickly on the NHL's heels the following season by signing Ulf Nilsson and Anders Hedberg.

The NHL had just expanded, and the advent of the WHA meant that teams needed to find more players somewhere, so a couple of the more innovative teams tapped into the European market. At first, the trend to bring over European players started out as just a trickle, and it took a long time before the Europeans begin to pour over from across the Atlantic.

Some of the great Soviets from the 1972 series against Canada would have been more than welcomed with open arms, especially sensational goaltender Vladislav Tretiak, but of course those players were under communist rule and weren't permitted to leave their country. Some Czechoslovakian players joined the NHL in the early 1980s, such as Peter, Anton, and Marian Stastny, and some of the older players were allowed to leave. But there were no Russians in the NHL until Sergei Priakin was allowed to sign with the Calgary Flames late in the 1988–89 season. Priakin was hardly the best the Russians had to offer, however, and he played only 46 games over three seasons, managing just three goals.

But for NHL teams, drafting and signing European players soon became a way of staying competitive. Soon dozens of Russian and Czech players joined the NHL. Whereas in 1973–74 there were only two Europeans in the NHL, in 1998–99 there were 149. Here is a breakdown of the ratios of Canadian, American, and European players on the 1998–99 opening-day rosters:

	Players in the NHL	Percentage
Canadians	409	62.3%
Europeans	149	22.7%
Americans	98	14.9%

The overall breakdown by country is as follows:

	Players in the NHL	Percentage
Canada	409	62.3%
USA	98	14.9%
Russia	42	6.4%
Czech Republic	36	5.5%
Sweden	33	5.0%
Finland	14	2.1%
Slovakia	5	0.8%
Latvia	4	0.6%
Ukraine	3	0.5%
England	3	0.5%
Poland	2	0.3%
Germany	2	0.3%
Lithuania	2	0.3%
Belarus	1	0.2%
South Africa	1	0.2%
Scotland	1	0.2%

I question the argument that European players joining the NHL takes jobs away from Canadian players. Back in 1972–73, there were only 16 teams and fewer than 350 players in the NHL; now, there are 28 teams and more than 600 players. Not only is there much more opportunity for Canadian players, there are far more Canadian players in the league than there were when Europeans first started to join the league. And with further expansion likely on the horizon, there will be even more jobs for Canadians.

European players are climbing the ranks of the amateur draft, however, and knocking Canadians out of the top 10 picks. And NHL teams are selecting Europeans more than ever. They can see the great value in their conditioning and speed, and the quality of the hockey programs in European countries.

In 1974, the first year that Europeans were drafted into the NHL, six were selected. The European invasion reached its peak in 1992, when 84 were selected. Most of the Europeans playing before 1988 came from Sweden and Finland. Because of the Russian political climate that restricted Russian players from joining the NHL until the late 1980s, only a few Russians were selected prior to the 1988 draft, but overall, more Russian players have been selected than from any other country. Here is a list showing the numbers of Europeans that have been drafted into the NHL from the four main European import regions, through 1999:

Russia (USSR/CIS)	**300**
Sweden	**293**
Czech Republic and Slovakia	**261**
Finland	**178**

In the first round of the 1999 amateur draft, several Europeans were selected early. In fact, players from 10 different countries were chosen in the first 28 selections. Only nine Canadians were picked, followed by four Americans, three each from Russia and the Czech Republic, two each from Sweden,

Finland, and Slovakia, and one from each of Ukraine, Belarus, and Switzerland. Here's how the draft went:

1	ATL	STEFAN, Patrik	Pribram, Czech Republic
2	VAN	SEDIN, Daniel	Ornskoldsvik, Sweden
3	VAN	SEDIN, Henrik	Ornskoldsvik, Sweden
4	NYR	BRENDL, Pavel	Opocno, Czech Republic
5	NYI	CONNOLLY, Tim	Syracuse, New York
6	NSH	FINLEY, Brian	Sault Ste. Marie, Ontario
7	WSH	BEECH, Kris	Salmon Arm, B.C.
8	NYI	PYATT, Taylor	Thunder Bay, Ontario
9	NYR	LUNDMARK, Jamie	Edmonton, Alberta
10	NYI	MEZEI, Branislav	Nitra, Slovakia
11	CGY	SAPRYKIN, Oleg	Moscow, Russia
12	FLA	SHVIDKI, Denis	Kharkov, Ukraine
13	EDM	RITA, Jani	Helsinki, Finland
14	SJ	JILLSON, Jeff	Providence, Rhode Island
15	PHX	KELMAN, Scott	Winnipeg, Manitoba
16	CAR	TANABE, David	Minneapolis, Minnesota
17	STL	JACKMAN, Barret	Trail, B.C.
18	PIT	KOLTSOV, Konstantin	Minsk, Belarus
19	PHX	SAFRONOV, Kiril	St. Petersburg, Russia
20	BUF	HEISTEN, Barrett	Anchorage, Alaska
21	BOS	BOYNTON, Nicholas	Nobleton, Ontario
22	PHI	OUELLET, Maxime	Beauport, Quebec
23	CHI	MCCARTHY, Steve	Trail, B.C.
24	TOR	CEREDA, Luca	Logano, Switzerland
25	COL	KULESHOV, Mihail	Perm, Russia
26	OTT	HAVLAT, Martin	Mlada Boleslav, Czech Republic
27	NJ	AHONEN, Ari	Jyvaskyla, Finland
28	NYI	KUDROC, Kristian	Micalovce, Slovakia

With so many Europeans now playing in the NHL, it makes the transition from European play to NHL play easier for those who cross the ocean and makes the adjustment to the North American lifestyle easier as well. Some of the earlier players didn't fare well when suddenly immersed in a foreign culture. Players who come over from other countries have so much to deal with all at once: culture shock, the language barrier (in some cases), homesickness, the more physical demands of the schedule and the style of play, the smaller ice surface, the different offensive systems and defensive systems to learn, increased personal freedom, boatloads of money, and sudden fame. That kind of adjustment would be hard enough for those of us who've experienced life, but remember that most of these players are 18- and 19-year-old kids who've likely never been away from home before.

Sudden wealth made life interesting for some of the European players in the 1970s and 1980s. Many bought fast cars, and others discovered the world of fast food. They were clearly impressed by the luxuries at their fingertips. This was a significant change in lifestyle for these players, and unfortunately hockey took a back seat for a while for some, until they were scared into making the adjustment, sometimes by team management, sometimes by the size of their waistline.

The longer schedule and increased amount of travel meant that many of these players were exhausted in the latter part of the season, and then, of course, they faced the rigours of the playoffs and a longer time away from home. The smaller ice surface meant they were much more likely to be hit in the corners and they couldn't take advantage of the free-wheeling style of play they'd become used to on the international hockey scene. These skilled skaters spent their entire playing careers setting up plays and pleasing the crowds with their offensive prowess. They weren't used to being hammered into the boards or being lured into a scrap by a goon, so it's easy to see why the European players shy away from more intense physical play. And they weren't used to being asked to knock around opposing players, either. It's not that they don't have the heart to play physically, it's just that the larger ice surface allows less opportunity for that kind of play, so few have become proficient at that part of the game.

Europeans often have a difficult time learning the defensive aspects of the North American game. They haven't learned to play the same way as our kids do, so taking responsibility for play in their own end is foreign to them, so to speak. That's why we often see Europeans with great offensive skills who are liabilities to their team because of their glaring defensive weaknesses. Remember Vladimir Ruzicka? He was a skilled Czech player who made some pretty plays for the Bruins in the early 1990s, but he was such a poor defensive player the team couldn't afford to let him play very much, and he was eventually sent packing.

That's not to say that some Europeans aren't excellent defensive players. There are several European players in the NHL who shine defensively, even better than Canadians and Americans who've learned defensive hockey since they first put on their skates. Take Finnish player Jere Lehtinen of the Dallas

Stars, for example. Lehtinen is one of the better defensive players in the game. He won the Selke Trophy as the NHL's best
defensive forward in both 1998 and 1999. Magnus Arvedson of
Sweden, a centre for the Ottawa Senators, is another premier
defensive player. He was a runner-up to Lehtinen in 1999 Selke
Trophy voting.

The growing pains appear to be over for European players.
For one thing, many of the younger players are coming over
earlier in their careers. They're learning the game on North
American ice, joining junior teams, and being drafted from
the Canadian Hockey League instead of from the teams they
normally would have joined in their home countries. Some opt
to play in the International Hockey League (IHL), too, although
players who've gone that route have shown less success than
junior draftees. Czech Radek Bonk of the Ottawa Senators,
for example, was the third player taken in the 1994 amateur
draft. His success in a season with Las Vegas of the IHL fuelled
his rise in the amateur draft rankings. Unfortunately, he has
failed to live up to expectations in five NHL seasons and has yet
to fill his projected role as one of the Senators' young leaders.

Another point that rankles critics of European players is that
at one time, NHL jobs were for Europeans to lose, rather than
win. If a team went through all the trouble of signing these
players and bringing them across the ocean (often surrepti-
tiously without permission of the home country's government),
they made sure that that player was in the starting lineup.
Do you remember former Leaf owner Harold Ballard's experiment with Czech star Miroslav Ihnacak in 1985–86? Ihnacak's

defection made big news. He had scored more than a point a game in Czechoslovakia. Leaf brass plugged the left winger directly into the Leaf lineup, and he struggled from the start. In 55 games as a Leaf over two seasons, he scored only 17 points. But the Leafs kept playing him because they'd made a big deal about adding him to the team. Ihnacak eventually moved on to the Detroit Red Wings, for whom he played but one game. Of course, other European players, such as Peter Stastny, jumped right into NHL starting lineups and never looked back.

Now, there seems to be a more natural order to things. Because there are so many European players contending for jobs in today's NHL, and because some of them have lived in North America, European players don't automatically make the team any more. Many now spend their time adjusting to the style of play in the minor professional leagues and earn spots on NHL rosters, in fair competition with the other players on the team. Previously, only a few had ever been asked to play in the minors. They either became starters, or if not given that opportunity would return to play in the European leagues.

The skill that many European players bring to the game has actually become a point of contention for their critics. Because they are better skaters and puck handlers than many North American players, it often seems to Canadian fans that these players are underachieving. Such fans (and the media) label these players as floaters because they don't seem to try. Alexei Kudashov, a Russian forward with the Leafs in 1993–94, was a skilled player, and everyone watching him play thought that he had the ability to tear the league apart. Yet to date he has scored only one NHL goal, and no assists.

Many fans still argue that European players are floaters, even though players such as Mats Sundin and Peter Forsberg have long since proven that supposition false. It's not only the fans and the media who perpetuate this myth, however. It has taken a while for NHL management to understand how the European players play, as well.

European players now have to earn spots on NHL teams rather than having jobs handed to them, a move that is better for all players in the league. It's better for the Europeans because they earn the respect of their teammates and fans (though they might already have proven themselves in the European leagues) and they earn a better understanding about what they have to do to be successful in the NHL. Other players in the league not only gain respect for these players because of their hard work, but they also compete with them for jobs, which can only make them strive to play better.

I observed how hockey was played in Europe in the late 1970s first-hand during my career and after, both as an official and as an instructor of officials. In 1979, I went to Kiev, Ukraine, with John D'Amico, a fellow NHL official, to participate in a hockey tournament. In the tournament, there were two teams from Russia, one from Poland, and one from Czechoslovakia. The National Hockey League sent us over to assist in their referee development program and to referee some games so they could watch us and learn our style of positioning, handling plays, making calls, etc.

It was one of my first experiences at refereeing a game between European teams. I was amazed at how they moved the puck around the bigger ice surface with such dexterity. They never seemed to waste a shot on net. Instead of flipping the puck in on the goalie and hoping for a rebound, they would circle the net and move around to get into the proper position, or better still they would try to draw an opponent out of position in order to take the best shot possible. And they didn't crowd around the net or hover at the blueline to do this like NHL players do — they used the full ice surface. They took advantage of the bigger ice surface, enjoying the room to roam. There wasn't a lot of body-checking in the game, and I found that I missed that aspect of the game. I think the North American game has got them on that one. Checking is an important part of the game, but on the bigger ice surface there was no need to contain players with tight checking.

When I watch the European players try to set up the play like they do overseas, I can see how they just become frustrated. That tactic doesn't work very well on our smaller ice surfaces. For example, for the 1992–93 season, St. Louis brought in three Russians to considerable fanfare: Igor Korolev, Vitali Karamnov, and Vitaly Prokhorov. They were miserable failures. They kept circling and circling, but never got anywhere. It just didn't work here. Korolev moved on to Winnipeg/Phoenix and Toronto, and no longer circles.

In 1983 I was invited by the Finnish Ice Hockey Federation to teach their senior referees the finer aspects of officiating for a few days at a sports camp at Verimaki, Finland, just outside of

Helsinki. I came to understand how their training methods differ from ours, and I could see how our training for officials would benefit from some of the aspects of their system. Those officials did a lot of dry-land training, which was unheard of in North America at the time. Now, however, many officials have incorporated dry-land training into their routines.

In 1984, after I had retired as an NHL referee, I received an invitation to referee in the oldest hockey tournament in all of Europe, the Spengler Cup tournament in Davos, Switzerland. The Spengler Cup features pretty good hockey, mostly from teams from different countries, including a number of Canadians playing on European teams. When the tourney, which always takes place at Christmas, was over, we travelled to Zurich and spent New Year's Eve dancing on the tables in a German pub with the Canadian team, which happened to have won the tournament that year.

Alan Eagleson, at the time director of the NHLPA, arranged for me to be invited to the 1985 World Championship of Hockey in Czechoslovakia. I became the first former professional referee to participate in the event and was honoured to do so. Besides, it was a special treat to get to visit Prague. The entire officiating team for the series spent three weeks in Prague refereeing games, living in an historic hotel in Old Prague, meeting many fine people, and dining in their classy restaurants along cobblestone streets that wind their way through alleys: another great memory for my memoirs.

The hockey at the World Championship was wide open, and I found it enjoyable, though some of the lesser-talented teams showed less zip in their style of play. I learned that despite the skills the European players possess, they, too, play a boring brand of hockey at times.

In all, I've spent a lot of time watching European hockey at variety of levels, and I've come to understand the differences in the way the game is played over there compared with the game over here. The European game does not feature nearly as much slam-bang hockey, but places an emphasis on playmaking. They don't run guys through the boards, but they still use their body to take the puck away from another player. They don't slap it into the opponents' end and then chase after it to get it back. There's more passing and puck handling in an effort to maintain possession and set up scoring plays.

European players are getting recognized for their NHL efforts at the awards ceremonies, as well. Other than Lehtinen's Selke win, European players came home with several awards at the 1999 ceremonies in Toronto. Jaromir Jagr won the Hart Trophy as the league's most valuable player, and the Art Ross, as the leading scorer. Teemu Selanne of the Mighty Ducks of Anaheim won the inaugural Rocket Richard Trophy as the leading goal scorer, and Dominik Hasek won the Vezina as the best goalie. Jagr, Selanne, and Hasek, as well Russians Sergei Fedorov and Sergei Samsonov, have each walked up to the podium in past years to collect hard-earned hardware. Peter Forsberg and Daniel Alfredsson won the Calder Trophy in 1994–95 and 1995–96.

The one area of the European play that hasn't risen to NHL standards is goaltending. Other than Hasek, few goalies from

European countries have had great success in the NHL or have proven themselves in international play. We all remember Tretiak's unbelievable work in the 1972 series, but think of other European goalies who've made the jump to the NHL and you'll be hard pressed to think of a good one (with the possible exception of the late Pelle Lindbergh). Really, there still aren't too many. Nikolai Khabibulin in Phoenix and Arturs Irbe in Carolina have distinguished themselves in recent years, but other than that, I draw a blank.

The main reason that European goaltenders haven't matched the success of the forwards and defencemen is that they've had to make a lot of adjustments to understand NHL play and be prepared. They can't get by on talent and instincts. They have to know the game. These goalies have reputations as poor puck handlers, but I can see why. On the larger ice surface of the European game, players do not take the puck behind the net as much because there's more room for them to skate, so they're not used to players setting up plays from behind the net, and players trying to dig the puck under their pads from behind.

As I noted earlier, European forwards work the puck to the centre of the ice in the attacking zone and try for a prime shot on net. Over here, the players blast the puck at the net from all different angles, so positioning tactics are a new aspect of the game for these goalies.

As well, North American players grow up with catching sports such as baseball, so they're far more practised in the skills of that aspect of the game. It seems to me that our goalies' hand-eye coordination is better.

Though the jury is still out on the goaltending skills of European netminders, there's no questioning European dominance at the offensive side of the game. On the 1999 All-Star teams, six of the 12 positions for the first and second team were filled by Europeans. On the first team were Peter Forsberg, Jaromir Jagr, Nicklas Lidstrom, and Dominik Hasek. The second All-Star team featured Alexei Yashin and Teemu Selanne. As well, seven of the top 12 scorers in the league in 1998–99 were European.

But despite the great offensive prowess shown by European players, they still lack leadership skills. They don't appear to take control of the dressing room. Some players do lead by example, however. Mats Sundin, captain of the Toronto Maple Leafs, is an excellent leader. He's not the classic NHL captain, but he's successful in getting his message across through the quality of his play and his devotion to the game. I think Europeans have not shown leadership skills as yet because they're still becoming comfortable with being minorities on a team. After all, the Canadian and American players get along just fine and are comfortable when one of their own steps up and tells it like it is, the Mark Messier style of captaining. Imagine how difficult it would be to jump in as one of just a few European players on a team, especially if you're not quite comfortable with the language, and tell a roomful of players to get their act together. I think that as Europeans become more comfortable with all aspects of our game (and as our game changes to reflect their contribution) Europeans will show their detractors that they're equally capable of leading an NHL team.

Fortunately, European imports are not expected to provide leadership in the dressing room right away. They're not used to that kind of pressure. In fact, many European teams bring in Canadian players to lead their teams. As I mentioned, Canadians have grown up in that kind of atmosphere. After all, the game is the single most defining feature of Canadian culture. From an early age, kids dream of one day skating around the ice hoisting the Stanley Cup. The kids grow up together through hockey and learn early who the leaders are and how to follow that leadership. It's a new facet of the game for many Europeans.

Critics of European players point to their lack of intensity. Though, as I've mentioned, I think a lot of that has to do with the ease with which they set up plays, there is some merit to their criticism. When I was refereeing in Europe, I noticed how intense the Russians and Czechs were, but I also noticed that the Swedes and Finns played a more laid-back style. The style of play of each country seemed to mirror the lifestyle of that particular country.

I think people misjudge the amount of passion and intensity European players have for hockey. The thing is, hockey is so important to Canadian kids, much more so than anywhere else in the world, where other sports are more popular. In many countries, people feel the same way about soccer, for example, as Canadians do about hockey. Canadians couldn't be expected to have the same passion that those countries hold for soccer, and those countries couldn't be expected to have the same passion that Canadians have for hockey. That's not to say that

Europeans don't love the game — they do, or they wouldn't be playing it. But Canadians kids are bred to play hockey.

Don't just take my word for it. Even Europeans recognize the heights that Canadian passion for hockey has reached, and how that translates into effective leadership skills. Jaromir Jagr, for one, has been widely quoted as saying the Pittsburgh Penguins have not been successful in the playoffs in recent years because they had too many Europeans on the team. This from a European.

Europeans have made substantial contributions to the NHL and to hockey in general. Their tremendous skills combined with the style of the North American game affords us the best the game has to offer. The surge of European players in the NHL has only benefitted our game. We get the best of both worlds. We get to see the best players in the world, not just North America. You can't ask for more than that.

There is little doubt that European players showcasing their talents and skills on North American ice is encouraging everyone, from the youngest hockey player all the way through to the top level and into hockey management, to want to learn to play the game better. If we don't soon learn the lesson the Europeans are teaching us each season, the Europeans will continue to dominate and may even some day outnumber the North American players. We can only benefit by learning how they play the game.

a wake-up call
for hockey

I'm 63 years old now, and for the most of those years, hockey has been a big part of my life.

From the days on the pond to my days playing in the first indoor arena in Milton, from natural ice to artificial ice, from stick boy to playing for the local junior, intermediate, and senior teams — all driven by my passion for and love of hockey.

When I was the manager of the local arena, I would make the ice, paint the lines on it, and flood it by hand (no Zambonis in those days) — I did everything. In fact, that's how I got started as a referee. I was always at the arena, always had my skates there, and was ready and willing to go if one of the officials didn't show up.

I was instrumental in bringing together the two local service clubs to form the Milton Minor Hockey Association.

I started up an industrial hockey league so players could play beyond minor hockey. I was the director and chief referee, and reffed most of the games, too. For fun, I still play hockey two or three times a week, and officiate the odd charity game.

My passion and enthusiasm for the game has not changed one little bit over the years. Yes, the crap that went on in the NHL in the 1970s made my job tough, and took away some of the fun. But through it all, my love of the game remains undiminished.

●

Taking responsibility is a quality of a good referee — the ability to see an infraction and react to it, and make the call. And as when I was a referee, calling it as I see it unfortunately irks some people. With my first book, *Calling the Shots*, I managed to offend some of those who were employed in the game at the time. It's too bad that those people didn't have the courage to speak up for the betterment of the game, but I doubt they would risk making waves in the hockey world.

In this book I've given my views about what's wrong with the game of hockey, and I've made some suggestions to fix the problems. I don't think anyone can wave a magic wand and right the wrongs of the game just like that. But I believe that if those in charge make a dedicated effort to change, and the parents of young players insist on it, the game can be much better, and more fun, too. And the long-term benefits of these changes, the development of talent, will appear eventually at the top levels of hockey.

I got my wake-up call about hockey after watching Canada's performance at the 1998 Olympics, but I'd seen the changes in the game during my time in hockey. I'd also read the hundreds of articles in magazines and newspapers and saw television reports that pointed out there was a problem with hockey. But few of these articles provided any answers. I have always believed that if you discuss a problem, you should also have suggestions to fix that problem, based on your experience and your gut feeling. And that's what I've done.

You see, kids just want to play hockey, and the adults playing hockey just want to play hockey, too. In the big leagues, the game is still the main attraction, and the entire event is geared toward entertainment — loud music, light shows, mascots, give-aways, souvenirs.

And when they play, they play with too much dedication to defensive hockey. If they keep slowing down the game and cut down further on scoring, eventually the game will come to a complete stop. Blocking the lanes, defensive traps, interference infractions, taking out opposition players, and other defensive tactics will become so dominant that the NHL will have to go to shoot-outs after 60 minutes of regulation and overtime just to get a 1–0 final. Do you think I'm exaggerating? If you look at how scoring in hockey these days continues to decrease, and you listen to coaches say that they want bigger, stronger players to shut down the opposition, you can see that I'm not exaggerating.

Hockey is such a simple game, but too many people are bringing their frustrations from their off-ice lives to the arena. Coaches, managers, and players are guilty of this. Even parents of kids in minor hockey are voicing their frustrations loud enough for everyone to hear. There are far too many incidents of abuse of referees, coaches, and players by parents these days. It would be better if those parents stayed home. I used to end a sports column I wrote in my earlier days with "Take, don't send your boy to the arena!" Today, I would change that to "Take your youngster to the arena and enjoy the game. Open your mouth only to cheer; otherwise, sit down and shut up! If you can't do that — stay home."

We've gone downhill as a hockey nation since the 1972 Canada-Soviet series. We've allowed the Broad Street Bully mentality to infect our players, coaches, and managers. They're simply performing in a system that demands the promotion of intimidation. But though they promote intimidation tactics and defensive traps, they're simply products of our system. I hope that executives at every level of hockey will create a new system, one that encourages coaches and managers to demonstrate the positive aspects of hockey — scoring, play-making, and having fun. Hockey is a sport in which young people develop not only as athletes but as individuals as well. The training they receive in hockey teaches them how to enjoy the game and gives them valuable tools to use in their personal lives. They should learn to win not by shutting down all attempts by the other team to score, but by handling the puck and making plays, like the European players do. And we've all seen recently how successful European players can be in our system.

A European player of stature once said that the future of hockey lies in a hybrid of the European player and Canadian player. You have to be a skilled, technical player, and be tough as well. Players have to understand that they need to develop their skills, while at the same time accept that people body check in hockey, and that you are going to get hit. But there is no need for constantly running players into the boards instead of playing the puck. That type of attitude and unnecessarily hard play scares some kids, who would rather quit the game than get knocked around all the time. If we allow normal contact as a part of playing the puck, I'm sure everybody would love to play hockey. Everybody enjoys a good body-check, but few enjoy brutality.

Over 10 years ago I first wrote about how the quality of hockey is going downhill, and since then it's only become worse. The beautiful plays are becoming fewer and fewer, and have given way to a bashing style of play — dump the puck into the corner, go in, hit everybody in sight, and get the puck back. Kick at the puck, cross-check, shoulder, elbow, hip-check — do what you can to free up that little piece of rubber. They occasionally move the puck in front of the net, where they wrestle some more, but mostly the action then moves to the other end of the rink and it starts all over again.

Hockey has changed, in some ways for the better. The players are bigger, the equipment is lighter and provides more protection, skates have better quality boots and steel in the blade, and the ice is better (but not everywhere, based on the number of complaints we heard during the Stanley Cup playoffs in 1999). Even coaching systems have changed. It used to be that one person would run the show from behind the bench. Now, coaches have two assistants with them on the players' bench and another assistant up in the press box using a headset to send information to the assistant coaches.

Even the dressing rooms are much different than in the old days. The pros have it made — workout areas, relaxation areas, dressing area, and get-away-from-the-press areas. Arenas now are modern facilities — no more dimly lit, ice-cold, shabby rinks. The dressing rooms are big enough now to house entire teams, so they don't have to squish together any more.

●

I have made several proposals in this book to change the game. I've suggested rule changes and developing an entirely new attitude toward the game in our young people. They need to grow into a new hockey environment, to play the game for fun, without losing out on the wonderful high of playing the game — the intensity, the ability to give and take hits, and most importantly, to play the game the way it's supposed to be played. Kids should learn how to stickhandle the puck, make passes, develop plays, and skate hard. And they should develop their personal skills and value systems on and off the ice. They need to develop self-discipline, learn teamwork, understand winning and losing and all the other aspects of hockey, and of life. Good, proper standards start with each community's hockey association, and include the coaches, who are a major influence on the players' lives.

We need to examine the role of fighting in hockey, as well. It's an unnecessary part of the game. Players who fight at any level should be given game misconducts instead of five-minute majors. But the players themselves are cutting down on the amount of fighting. The goon mentality still exists, and that may never disappear entirely because teams will always wait for the other team to cut their goons first. So be prepared to see someone get pummeled the next time you watch a hockey game. You might even see a player's career ended during a fight.

We need to get rid of other kinds of violence in hockey as well — the intimidating tactics, the scrums, the taunts and slurs. We can start to remove these aspects of the game by losing our win-at-all-costs attitude. The referees and the coaches should meet off the ice to clear the air, and to eliminate carrying over disputes from game to game.

I hope, for the sake of hockey, that the people in charge allow the game to open up, that they stop promoting defensive tactics that slow hockey to a standstill. Instead, they should promote offensive prowess. The media would pick up on the quality of play rather than writing about the thugs.

I issue a challenge to you, whether reader, player, coach, manager, league executive, parent, referee, or fan, to work together to make hockey the best it can be. I'm a big fan of the game, and while I know that we can never go back to the good old days, if there ever really were any, I also know that the game can be far better than what we've seen in recent years.

So there you have it, folks. On my journey through the past, present, and future of hockey, and in voicing my concerns for hockey, I've come up with a blueprint for recapturing hockey's greatness:

- We need to take a close look at kids' hockey, at the violence and fighting in the game in particular. Parents should look at their role in their children's development as players, and make hockey a positive experience for them.
- Cut down on the defensive tactics, and open up the game. More scoring means more excitement.
- Eliminate fighting.
- Learn from hockey's past. There was a lot of good hockey in the Original Six era.
- Give the officials the guidance and support they need to make the right calls.
  Get salaries under control. The more money players make, it seems the less involved they become in team effort.
- Improve relations between the media and the players. The media need to focus on the good (not on digging up dirt), and the players need to make themselves available for comment.
- Slow down expansion, or stop it altogether. There simply aren't enough quality players to go around. Expansion has gone into overtime.
- Learn from those who play hockey just for the fun of it.
- The Europeans are here to stay, so get used to it. They're

showing us how hockey should be played — with skill and finesse, not cross-checks and high sticks.

- Think of hockey's greats — Wayne Gretzky, Mario Lemieux, Jean Beliveau, Bobby Orr, Bobby Hull, Vladislav Tretiak, Darryl Sittler, Frank Mahovlich, Guy Lafleur — all those who shared their love and dedication for the game. We can only hope that our children can someday match their passion for hockey.

It's time to get out the skates and equipment for another game now, right after I watch last night's hockey highlights for the umpteenth time.

Have a good one!

If you would like to comment on *The Good of the Game* or share your hockey memories, please contact me by e-mail at hockey@brucehood.com or care of my publisher. I welcome your opinions.